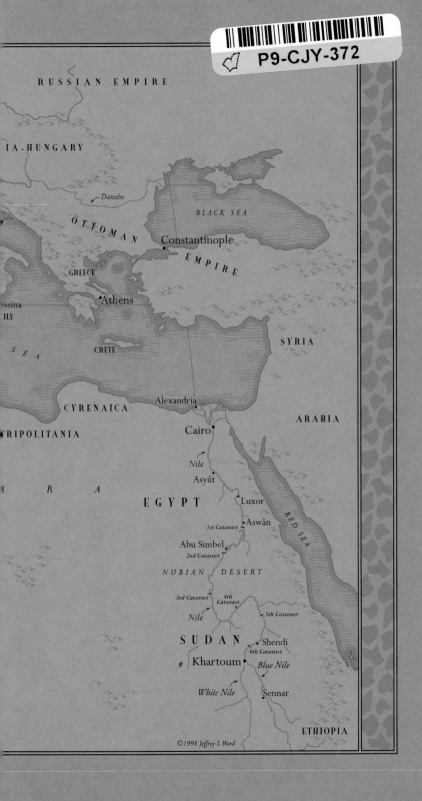

P9-CJY-372

RUSSIAN EMPIRE

IA-HUNGARY

Danube

OTTOMAN

BLACK SEA

Constantinople

EMPIRE

GREECE

•Athens

essina
ILY

SEA

CRETE

SYRIA

CYRENAICA

Alexandria

ARABIA

TRIPOLITANIA

Cairo•

Nile

R A

Asyût

EGYPT

Luxor

Aswân

1st Cataract

RED SEA

Abu Simbel
2nd Cataract

NUBIAN DESERT

3rd Cataract 4th
Cataract

5th Cataract

Nile

SUDAN •Shendi
6th Cataract

Khartoum• *Blue Nile*

White Nile Sennar

ETHIOPIA

©1998 Jeffrey L. Ward

Zarafa

Zarafa

*A Giraffe's True Story,
from Deep in Africa
to the Heart of Paris*

Michael Allin

Walker and Company
New York

First published in the United States of America in 1998
by Walker Publishing Company, Inc.

Library of Congress Cataloging-in-Publication Data
Allin, Michael, 1944–
Zarafa : a giraffe's true story, from deep in Africa to the
heart of Paris / Michael Allin.
p.   cm.
Includes index.
ISBN 0-8027-1339-4 (hardcover)
1. Giraffe—France—Biography.
2. Zoo animals—France—
History—19th century.   I. Title.
QL737.U56A53   1998
599.638'092'9—dc21
[B]   98-23091
CIP

Book design by M.J. DiMassi

Printed in the United States of America
2   4   6   8   10   9   7   5   3   1

This book is for
Jack Allin

Contents

Prologue

Through a hole in the wall
Of the Jardin des Plantes
We come to go round
The animals for the last time . . .
— *James Dickey*, "Goodbye to Serpents"

L IVES AGO, those lines were the first place I ever saw the words *Jardin des Plantes*. "Goodbye to Serpents" is a poem about an American father and son whose final visit to the old Paris zoo, located in the park that is le Jardin des Plantes, becomes their farewell to Europe.

I loved the poem for its snakes in my imagined paradise of Paris, and for the lucky little son in it, and for its searching irony that was quintessential Jim Dickey: the irony that the poet's disconnection with what he is seeing dogs him and drives him to find his own relationship with it. "The hardest thing in the world," Jim was always saying, "is to make a mountain out of a molehill."

Ever since first reading "Goodbye to Serpents," I have sought out any mention of le Jardin des

Plantes. As a university student working first in the
college library, then in a bookstore, I developed a
ritual of checking for le Jardin, along with my hand-
ful of other obsessions, in every book that had an
index. Long before I ever saw it, I knew that the
oldest tree in Paris has grown in le Jardin since it
was founded in 1635; and that la Rotonde is the
menagerie's oldest and most beautiful building, designed to replicate the cross of the Napoleonic Legion of Honor; and that the menagerie, which is the
world's oldest municipal zoo, was started with animals rescued from the mobs of the French Revolution.

It took me years to get to Paris. My first morning
finally there in 1977, I took my wife to see le Jardin
des Plantes and say hello to the serpents. It was perfect spring, sunny and warm. The intricate gardens
were full of flowers. The endless *allées* of plane trees
and horse chestnuts were magnificent with their new
leaves. But the old art nouveau serpentarium was
shabby and sad. The snakes were geriatric. My pilgrimage was a disappointment. Until a zookeeper ran
through, yelling, "On ferme! On ferme! Closing!"
and herded the few of us outside and around to a
big window looking into the enclosure of the python.

The python was as thick around as my thigh and
had climbed vertically most of its fifteen feet up an
inside edge of the window. Its head was up out of
sight, and we did not realize at first that it was
a snake because its body was so big and gleaming

dark like a wet tree. A three- or four-inch slit in the snake, perfectly positioned for spectating, widened, and out of it we watched eggs slowly appear, one by one, as asymmetrical and irregular as stones, no two alike.

At the inside door of the python's enclosure, two khaki-uniformed zookeepers and a blond woman in a white laboratory smock over a yellow dress were beside themselves with excitement. I have no idea how much time went by; but when the eggs stopped coming, we had counted seventeen.

Then, after an animated consultation, the two very nervous keepers climbed through the door into the enclosure, one with a gunnysack that he held up at full arm's length around the python's head, struggling to hold it as the gigantic snake began to writhe, while the other man handed the eggs out to the blond woman, who gathered them in her smock like a farmer's wife in her apron. When she had them all in her standing lap, the egg-gathering keeper exited and got ready to close the glass door of the enclosure as fast as he could after the man with the gunnysack let it drop and leaped away from the snake.

The two men and the woman disappeared until they emerged hurrying in a tight group, their six hands all carrying her smock full of eggs, out of the serpentarium and across the gravel and into another building.

The snake slithered down onto the floor, huge-headed and even more awesome in its horizontal length as it searched around and around the cage.

⟋

AFTER I WAS thus granted experiential ownership of le Jardin des Plantes, my obsession with it became proprietary. And one day, after twenty-five years of checking indexes, I found an astonishing paragraph in the *New Yorker* about a giraffe that had arrived at le Jardin in 1827—astonishing because this first giraffe ever seen in France, after sailing from Egypt, had walked all the way from Marseille to Paris.

It was a simple story, or so I thought at first, based upon the innocently exotic and fairy-tale image of a giraffe—a royal gift from Muhammad Ali, the Ottoman viceroy of Egypt, to King Charles X of France—strolling through the glorious French countryside in spring.

Researching the giraffe over the next decade, I found her story told and retold—by scientists, journalists, historians, novelists and authors of childrens' books, cartoonists and painters—accruing an amazement of details that were hopelessly unreliable. Intending to treat it as fiction, though, I felt no need to seek the truth. The giraffe's chroniclers, myself included, had fallen in love with her story, myths and all; and as by a pharaoh's curse on tomb robbers, we were spellbound to convey wonder instead of facts.

Giraffe, girafe, giraffa (English, French, Italian)—all derive from the Arabic *zerafa,* a phonetic variant of *zarafa,* which means "charming" or "lovely one." I named the giraffe Zarafa and imagined her wading through a field of sunflowers somewhere in France. But as I learned more about the extraordinary achievement of her arrival in Paris, the scattered facts became too impressive to fictionalize. And as the humans involved with the giraffe's journey emerged in my research as real-life figures, the fairy tale kept backing up into ever more fascinating history.

France's first giraffe was the brainchild in 1824 of Bernardino Drovetti, French consul general in Egypt and indispensable private adviser to Muhammad Ali. The viceroy was about to become unpopular in Europe for his war against the Greeks, and Drovetti's suggested gift of a giraffe was intended to befriend Charles X, who had become the king of France that year.

Drovetti and the viceroy were both expatriate adventurers who had come to Egypt at the turn of the nineteenth century: Drovetti was a young Italian soldier turned French bureaucrat; Muhammad Ali was an Albanian mercenary in the Ottoman Turkish army. Both men were, like the giraffe, charming and deadly in their contradictions.

Muhammad Ali sent his son and thousands of

other Arabs to be educated in Europe, while financing his impressive modernization of Egypt with the African slave trade and confiscatory taxation of his subjects. Drovetti, officially a diplomat, made a fortune trafficking in exotic animals, Egyptian antiquities, mummies by the pound, and whatever else his wealthy European clients desired.

Drovetti was the classic entrepreneurial middleman, an expert at turning royal gratitude to his own financial advantage. His long relationship with the viceroy made him the most powerful European in Egypt. As the first wholesale tomb robber of modern Egyptology, Drovetti was ingratiating to his patrons and dangerous to his competitors. His career in Egypt spanned almost thirty years, and his archaeological removals became the great museum collections now in Turin and Paris and Berlin.

Zarafa's walk from Marseille to Paris turned out to be but the finale to a journey she had begun 4,000 miles and two years before in central Africa. Captured as a calf in the Ethiopian highlands by Arab hunters, she had been packed on a camel to Sennar and shipped down the Blue Nile to be raised in Khartoum. From Khartoum she had traveled the harrowing slave trail down the entire length of the Nile, nearly 2,000 miles to Cairo and Alexandria—none of the various versions agreed as to how—before sailing across the Mediterranean.

Zarafa's survival was ensured by fear of the viceroy's wrath and by Drovetti's experience in shipping

African animals to Europe. In Alexandria, Drovetti
put his Arab groom, Hassan, in charge of her journey
to Paris and sent along his Sudanese servant, Atir, to
assist. They were three weeks on the Mediterranean,
another week waiting off Marseille—thirty-two days
in all—during which the giraffe rode standing among
the other animals in the hold with her long neck and
head protruding through a hole cut in the deck.

While bureaucrats in Marseille and Paris squab-
bled over who was responsible for the giraffe's
expenses, the prefect of Marseille doted on her,
constructing a stable especially for her on the
grounds of his mansion and bringing her there
through the city late at night to avoid the crowds.
Hassan and Atir wintered in the stable with her,
training her to follow milk cows on fair-weather con-
stitutionals. These lengthening walks out into the
countryside around Marseille eventually convinced
the prefect and Hassan that the giraffe could walk to
Paris in short daily treks.

The procession set out on May 20, 1827, led by
no less than Étienne Geoffroy Saint-Hilaire, one of
the foremost scientists of his time. In 1793, when
the French Revolution had created the National Museum of Natural History, Saint-Hilaire, at twenty-
one, had been the youngest of its twelve founding
professors. It was Saint-Hilaire who had started the
Paris zoo with animals saved from the mobs that had
attacked the royal menagerie at Versailles. Before he
was thirty, he had been among the heroic *corps des*

savants that accompanied Napoleon's Egyptian campaign in 1798 and was stranded there with the army
for three years.

Now fifty-five and suffering from gout and rheumatism, Saint-Hilaire was a living legend, a grand
and improbable eminence to make this journey with
the giraffe on foot. In Marseille he hired an Arab
urchin named Youssef, the bilingual son of Egyptian
refugees, to serve as his aide and translator with Hassan and Atir.

Marseille to Paris in May and June of 1827 was a
550-mile parade, during which the giraffe became
such a never-seen-before attraction that crowds rioted
around her. People came out of their fields and vineyards and distant villages to marvel at this living myth-
ological combination of creatures—a gentle and
mysterious sort of horned camel whose hump had
been straightened by stretching its neck, with legs as
tall as a man and the cloven hoofs of a cow, and
markings like a leopard or a maze of lightning, and
that startling blue-black snake of a twenty-inch
tongue. During the journey, Saint-Hilaire's health
deteriorated, and officials in Paris ignored his concern about the increasing crowds. By the time the
convoy reached Lyon, the giraffe was so famous that
30,000 people turned out to see her. In Paris she
was paraded through the city and presented to the
king.

This conclusion to Zarafa's travels was only the

beginning of the sensation she became in Paris, where glamorous women imitated her with their hair styled high, *à la Girafe,* and in the streets and salons, men wore fashionably *giraffique* hats and ties. Now remembered as a beautiful but vague legend, France's first living giraffe was a national icon, the envy of Europe, the subject of songs and poems, vaudeville skits and political allegories, the namesake of public squares and streets and inns and even a form of influenza.

Atir remained in Paris with Zarafa, becoming renowned as the Arab who lived with the giraffe in her enclosure at le Jardin des Plantes. Two ladders took him up to a mezzanine, where he slept within scratching reach of her head. Grooming her was his daily public performance. By night, he was also famous as a neighborhood ladies' man.

IN THE FALL OF 1996, I set out to retrace Zarafa's journey. On Thanksgiving Day, I was in Sennar on the Blue Nile. Below the town the river bends, widening to the north, but there is nothing left of the landing where Zarafa and so many hundreds of thousands of human captives embarked for Khartoum. The French explorer Frédéric Cailliaud saw giraffes at Sennar in 1821. Arab slavers and hunters soon depopulated them, so that only three years later,

Zarafa was captured 200 miles away. As I followed the Blue Nile from Sennar to Khartoum and on down the Nile into Egypt, the seasonal logic of the river made it clear to me that Zarafa would have sailed easily all the way to Alexandria.

In Africa there are no written records of Zarafa until Cairo. These were forgotten until 1938, when the archives of Muhammad Ali were discovered in the snake-infested cellars beneath his tomb at the Citadel. Every official word he had spoken during his reign of more than forty years had been transcribed into Arabic and saved. King Farouk, Egypt's last ruling descendant of Muhammad Ali, ordered an inventory that year of these documents, among which were found the viceroy's orders regarding "the giraffe from Sennar." During the inventory, these orders were not translated from Arabic; they were only described to a European journalist, who, with great love and inaccuracy, ultimately reminded France of the story of its first giraffe.

From Sennar to Khartoum and down the Nile to Cairo and Alexandria and across the Mediterranean, this journalist's invaluable inaccuracies led me at last to treasure buried in the archives of Marseille—a dusty, ribbon-tied cache of 170-year-old official and unofficial letters, ministerial reports and memos, and detailed day-to-day invoices of the giraffe's winter in Marseille and subsequent spring journey to Paris.

This miraculous find revealed firsthand accounts

of that part of her story, while old newspapers in Lyon provided further eyewitness reports of the tumult that greeted "the beautiful Egyptian" and her exotic Arab handlers. The same newspapers were shrill with anti-Islamic news of Muhammad Ali's war on the Greeks. Zarafa came to life with the times she lived in, and her story elaborated into a kaleidoscope of historical connections.

The giraffe was a royal gift intended to link Egypt and France. She was an emissary from another world whose journey, like the Nile itself, threaded distant and unimaginably disparate places. But the cast of characters along her way, and the history they gather and bring into focus around her, are as astonishing as her walk to Paris. Drovetti *is* Egyptology, which began with Napoleon's invasion in 1798; that, in turn, set the stage for Muhammad Ali, the renaissance barbarian whose enamored admiration for the French not only modernized Egypt but unlocked its ancient past. From beginning to end, and on every level, Zarafa's story is one of incongruous encounters—as complicated as the African slave trade meeting the European Enlightenment, and as deceptively simple as the White Nile and the Blue Nile contending into the Nile.

1
Two Africas

$\sim$

AT KHARTOUM, Shambat Bridge now spans
the very beginning of the Nile. Just south of
the bridge is the pointed tip of densely
wooded Tuti Island, around which the White Nile
and the Blue Nile meet without yet mixing, converg-
ing only their widths here into the new river.

The White Nile on the Omdurman side to the
west is wider and slower, 2,000 miles from its source
in Lake Victoria on the equator. The Blue Nile has
traveled only half as far, easing deceptively south as
the heart-shaping point of Lake Tana before swinging
west and north to roller-coaster down out of Ethiopia. The vigor of the Blue Nile keeps it free of the
parasitical flatworm that causes bilharzia (also called
snail fever), the main symptom of which is the dys-

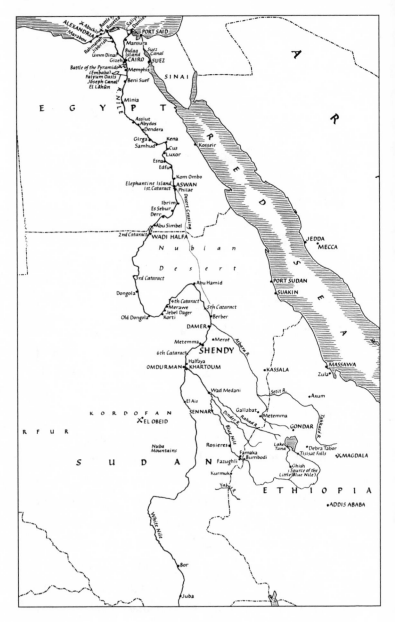

Map of the Nile

entery that has plagued the White Nile since the
Third World was the First World.

In Zarafa's time and before, until the dams
upriver from Sennar subdued the Blue Nile, its
wilder and more powerful summer flood blocked the
White Nile to a standstill at the southern end of Tuti
Island. Eighty-five percent of the annual inundation
of the Nile came from the Blue Nile, fecundating
desert Egypt with the black silt of the Ethiopian
highlands.

Even today with the dams on both rivers, the
Blue Nile rises roiling dark in summer—August is
still the month of flood watch in Khartoum—while
the White Nile, no longer impeded, creeps wider,
too slowly to lose its milky blue. The two rivers are
then at their ultimate contrast of color and tempera-
ment, two distant Africas coming together and clash-
ing for miles before gradually merging.

In the fall their disparity subsides to two gently
different currents rippling side by side under Shambat Bridge, and the deeper, faster Blue Nile really is
blue. Meeting it, the White Nile seems faded, older;
half a mile wide even at year's ebb, it is so shallow
off Tuti Island that fishermen at first and last light
step out of their boats and walk their nets mid-
stream.

On the east bank south of Tuti Island is the
promontory, sided by both rivers, upon which the
Egyptian Turks established their military outpost that

became Khartoum. The name Khartoum derives
from the Arabic word for an elephant's trunk, sup-
posed by Western historians and guidebooks to describe the shape of the promontory. But *elephant
trunk* does not in fact refer to the promontory. A
village of river Arabs, the Mahas, had occupied this
jutting corner of land between the two Niles for at
least a couple of centuries before the Turks founded
their capital here in 1824. The oldest of the seven
quarters of the Mahas' village was known by its *khartoum*—a specific outcropping rock that is still there
near the Mahas' seventeenth-century mosque, the
city's earliest, just east of the promontory—and the
Turks took the name of this quarter for their town.

The Mahas lived in villages all along the looping
Upper Nile in Sudan and Nubia, and wherever they
found the topographical fact of this type of rock protruding near or out of water, all these places carried
the name *khartoum*. Long before the Turks, there
were seven *khartoums* south of Kalabsha.

Looping north through Sudan for 1,000 miles,
the Nile was blocked before the dams of the twentieth century by the six Cataracts between Khartoum
and Aswân. (Today there are only five; the Second
Cataract at the Egyptian-Sudanese border is now at
the bottom of Lake Nasser.) The Cataracts are not
actually waterfalls, but natural dams of elephant-gray
rock that used to be more or less submerged during
the summer floods. Until the Turkish garrisons se-
cured the Upper Nile in the early 1820s, the Cata-

racts did not make the river unnavigable so much as dangerous to portage because of the Mahas and other tribes of Muslim warriors who lived along the banks.

In the centuries before the Turks, these tribes preyed upon the caravans that linked central Africa with Cairo and the world. Seeking safety in numbers, the caravans were huge amalgamations of strangers and traders, some with whole families traveling for years from market to market, caravan to caravan back and forth across Africa and the Middle East and even all the way to China.

The most feared of the Muslim tribes along the Nile were the Shaqiya between the Fourth and Fifth Cataracts. To avoid them, the north-south caravans left the Nile between Berber and Aswân for 400 waterless do-or-die miles across the Sahara. The desert crossing was kept well marked by the skeletons of camels that were butchered as they failed along the way and were left with their skulls facing toward Mecca. The humans unable to continue were robbed by their companions and abandoned to die or be killed first by marauders who followed in wait.

For centuries the two major caravan routes across Africa—Sennar to the Mediterranean, Timbuktu to the Red Sea—were slave trails to the successive civilizations of East and West and over time on to the Americas. The two routes intersected in the slave market at Shendi just north of the southernmost Cataract.

Since before climatic changes created the Sahara

8,000 years ago—when giraffes and elephants and other animals ranged the savanna clear to the Mediterranean—humans have lived along the loops of the Upper Nile. The animals retreated south before the arid heat that has, until now, preserved the monuments of ancient Egypt. But in Nubia and Sudan, on either side of the river, man remained in a narrow oasis hundreds of miles long, sustained by an extensive irrigation system of waterwheels and sweeps that captured the Nile bucket by bucket.

The residents of the ancient villages along the river between the six Cataracts harvested crops and orchards and the forests of yellow-blooming acacias. The throat-burning resin in acacia wood is resistant to insects and moisture, and, in addition to using the wood for charcoal, the Nubians turned it into their boats, waterwheels, and sweeps. Dongola, the capital of this ancient kingdom, is still famous for its groves of date palms. Downriver from Dongola, there is archaeological evidence that the early Nubians eventually became powerful enough to take slaves from among their former masters, the pharaonic Egyptians; and that these Egyptian captives, as though ironically cursed by their slaving ancestors, were buried alive with the corpses of their Nubian owners.

Perhaps the Upper Nile's age-old history as a slave route is responsible, at least in part, for the sweet dignity, watchful and tinged with melancholy, that so many Sudanese today seem to share. The Republic of Sudan, only forty years independent and the largest country in Africa, has always been the ethnic and climatic crossroads of the continent. Just as desert blends into rain forest 1,000 miles to the south, White Africa and Black Africa meet and meld in Sudan, darkening through the Nubians of the Sahara to the dazzling ebony Nuer and Dinka toward the equator.

The most prominent feature on a map of Sudan is the huge snaking *S* the Nile makes from Khartoum to the Egyptian border. *S* for *Sudan*, which, by a topographical-etymological coincidence, is an Arabic word for the "blackness" of the natives that the early Muslims encountered along the Upper Nile. *S* for *slaves*.

IT WAS MUHAMMAD ALI's slave trade that brought the Arabs who captured and cared so well for Zarafa. What a mysterious journey it must have been for human and animal captives alike, out of primeval Africa down the Nile through an otherworldly desert. At Abu Simbel, between the Second and First Cataracts, the four colossal pharaohs carved out of the cliff on the west bank—each with its huge negroid face of Rameses II, looking more like the captives than the captors aboard the passing feluccas—had only recently been discovered and excavated. At Cairo the Sphinx, also negroid, stared neck-deep in

sand, bodiless until the twentieth century. Most of
ancient Egypt still lay buried either in the desert or,
like the temples of Luxor and Karnak, in centuries
of human rubble thirty feet deep. What was visible
in Zarafa's time, from Abu Simbel in the south to
the Sphinx in the north, inspired travelers on the
Nile to fantasize that they had entered the land of an
extinct race of giants.

Egyptology began, as does the story of Muhammad Ali and the giraffe he sent to Paris, with Napoleon's invasion of Egypt. Twenty-eight years before
Zarafa journeyed down the Nile, French troops had
left their graffiti on the ancient monuments and
abandoned the grand disaster of their conquest. The
wreckage of their ships still littered the beach when
Zarafa arrived at Alexandria. By then, though, the
debris of the expedition's military defeat had become
a memorial to its unparalleled intellectual success,
and France and Egypt had united in mutual fascination.

2

A Fascinating
Nightmare

WE OWE OUR retrieval of ancient Egypt
to Napoleon and to the soldiers and savants of his expedition in 1798. The
eighteenth-century Enlightenment faith in the collective human mind had fired democratic revolutions
in America and France, and this military and scientific invasion of another world was the first great adventure of the new era.

When the French beheaded King Louis XVI on
January 21, 1793, Napoleon was twenty-three, a junior officer of artillery given to pondering suicide
late at night along the Seine. Exactly five years later,
General Napoleon had led his country to triumph in
the wars brought on by the Revolution. France had
stood alone against all of Europe, and Napoleon was
the inspiration of a nation of heroes.

The new French republic, rich from the young general's brilliant victories in Italy and Austria, gratefully offered him command of a new army forming at Brest to invade England. Napoleon rejected that invasion, considering it impossible against the superior sea power of the British. He proposed, however, that the preparations at Brest be continued in order to divert allied British and Spanish naval forces away from the Mediterranean. This would enable a large second French army to embark secretly from various Mediterranean ports, then assemble at sea and sail to Egypt, conquer its way by land from there through the Middle East, and ultimately capture the jewel of the British Empire, India.

The government delayed approval of the audacious plan until April 1798, but Napoleon's organizational genius had the Grand Army of the Orient ready to sail by the third week in May from Toulon, Genoa, Ajaccio, and Civitavecchia. The secrecy of the operation was so tight that almost all of the tens of thousands of people involved had no idea where they were headed. Neither did they care, such was their disciplined loyalty to Napoleon.

Dominique-Vivant Denon, Napoleon's documentarian, sailed with the main force from Toulon and described the combined flotilla of almost 400 ships as a floating city that covered the sea. In the glow of sunset, the surrounding skyline of sails became a gilded vision of the domes and spires of Venice—as though that unique city where East meets West had allegorically launched itself to follow Napoleon's star to the Orient. His star also had its attendant wise men in the 154 French savants accompanying the army. Only those aboard the flagship, *l'Orient,* knew that the twenty-eight-year-old commander of this immense adventure was seasick for most of the voyage.

The ruse at Brest was effective; England and Spain were lax in their surveillance of the Mediterranean, convinced that the French ships would head west for the Atlantic via Gibraltar to join the imminent invasion of England. Napoleon's fleet avoided enemy contact and, after taking Malta and leaving 4,000 troops to hold it, arrived at Alexandria on July 1.

Napoleon himself led a vanguard of 5,000 men ashore to take the garrison by night and ensure an unopposed landing. During the next few days, the remaining 29,000 troops were off-loaded with their supplies and armament. Knowing that his ships were sitting targets if the British appeared, Napoleon ordered the fleet to sail to the safety of Corfu after it had completed landing matériel. On July 7 he and the army began their forced march across the desert toward Cairo and the Mamelukes.

The Mamelukes were a bizarre cultural phenomenon of early Islam. Originally a caste of non-Arab Eurasian slaves—exclusively boys, not captured but sold into glory by their nomadic parents—they were trained to serve as professional soldiers in the armies of Muslim rulers. By the thirteenth century these blue-eyed warrior slaves—*Mameluke* is Arabic for "one possessed"—had developed their own closed society, loyal only to the highest bidder. In 1258 Genghis Khan's Mongols sacked Baghdad, then the capital of the Islamic Empire. Mamelukes elsewhere took the opportunity to usurp their consequently weakened masters and soon ruled much of the Middle East, most formidably in Egypt. Among them, the price they had brought as children was a matter of status and pride. Bibars, the first Mameluke sultan of Egypt, was also known as the Thousander after the amount for which he had traded hands.

Savage and theatrical fighters devoted to factional intrigue and violence, unmarried and homosexual, replenishing their ranks in turn with young Eurasian slaves of their own, the Egyptian Mamelukes became a dissolute Eastern equivalent of the medieval knights of Europe, whom they defeated in the Seventh Crusade of 1248–54. After an initial victory at Damietta, the French king Louis IX and his entire army of 15,000 to 25,000 Crusaders were captured and held for ransom.

Egypt's ruling class of 20,000 Mamelukes remained independent even after subjugation into the Ottoman Empire in 1517. Cairo paid tribute to Constantinople, but the native population was brutally exploited by the Mamelukes. They lived lavishly,

Mameluke cavalryman

with such incongruous elegance that European de-
scriptions generally sound as though their authors
were shocked by the orgy but amazed by the decor.
Stanley Lane-Pool, a late-nineteenth-century English
Orientalist, wrote of the Mamelukes: "A band of
lawless adventurers, slaves in origin, butchers by
choice, bloodthirsty, and too often treacherous,
these slave kings had a keen appreciation for the arts
which would have done credit to the most civilized
ruler that ever sat on a constitutional throne."

Napoleon, too, admired his first sight of an advance force of 3,000 Mamelukes who were brave
enough to skirmish with his vastly outnumbering

army: "A splendid body of mounted men, all gleaming with gold and silver, armed with the best London carbines and pistols, and the best sabers of the East, riding perhaps the best horses on the Continent."

But eleven days later at the Battle of the Pyramids on July 21, 1798, 6,000 Mameluke cavalry were no match for French artillery and discipline under fire. Denon described the final suicidal charge of the Mamelukes: "The finest cavalry of the Orient, perhaps of the entire world, threw itself against a small corps bristling with bayonets; there were those of them whose clothing was set aflame by the fire of our musketry."

Many of the retreating Mamelukes drowned in the Nile, while survivors scattered upriver and into the desert. Cairo surrendered the next day, presenting Napoleon with the keys to the city. Five hundred years of Mameluke rule of Egypt had ended literally overnight.

Meanwhile, at Alexandria, most of the French flotilla had sailed away. But bad weather had closed in and detained the guarding warships long enough for the British to find them. On August 1, eleven days after the Battle of the Pyramids, British ships under the command of one-eyed, one-armed Rear Admiral Horatio Nelson trapped and destroyed the French fleet in the Bay of Abukir. The wreckage littered twelve miles of beach, where it remained for decades.

Only four of Napoleon's warships escaped destruction at Abukir. As quickly as the Mamelukes had lost Egypt, the French were stranded in their conquest. The British navy, with a loss of only 218 dead and 672 wounded sailors, had effectively captured Napoleon and his 34,000 troops. At home, the peace won by his victories became unenforceable, and within months a weakened, chaotic France was back at war with nearly all of Europe.

⌒

EGYPT, FOR NAPOLEON, became a long fascinating nightmare, which he described as "the most delightful [time] of my life . . . free from the wearisome restraints of civilization." Over the next year in Africa and the Middle East, the contradictions of his genius emerged in full force, to be later admired and emulated by Muhammad Ali.

In Cairo Napoleon ate with his fingers on the floor of his sumptuously cushioned palace. He wore a turban and rode a camel that was later stuffed and displayed for years in a provincial museum in France.

While in Egypt Napoleon converted to Islam as a matter of diplomatic practicality and included local Arab intellectuals with his French savants in their scientific academy, l'Institut d'Égypte. The physicist Joseph Fourier was elected "perpetual secretary" of its forty-eight chairmen, one of whom was twenty-six-year-old Étienne Geoffroy Saint-Hilaire. Napo-

Napoleon in Cairo

leon was so honored by his own election to their
chair of mathematics that he never missed a meeting.

After three months of enlightened French occupation, though, Cairo erupted in revolt, which Napoleon
suppressed by decapitating any armed insurgent.
Then, in Syria, logistically unable to take prisoners of
all who surrendered after his victory at Jaffa, Napoleon
and his officers spared 300 and ordered execution of
the remaining 2,441 Turkish soldiers and civilians, at
first by shooting, then by bayonet to save ammunition.

In August 1799, when Napoleon had just turned
thirty, the political chaos in Paris forced him to
abandon his army in Egypt. He quit Cairo with only

his top generals and a few of his intellectuals, most of whom were unaware until they had embarked at Alexandria that they were running the British blockade back to France.

Napoleon was already gone when his letter informed General Jean-Baptiste Kléber that he had been left in command of the army in Egypt. Furious at Napoleon's secret departure, Kléber exclaimed, "That dumdum has left us with our breeches full of shit, we are going to return to Europe and apply them to his face!" Napoleon ordered Kléber to wait for reinforcements from France; if they had not arrived in nine months, or if 1,500 men died of the plague, Kléber was empowered to surrender. Kléber waited four months, then refused to subject his men to further hardship and capitulated to the British-Turkish alliance.

Britain and France had been at war since February 1, 1793, eleven days after Louis XVI was beheaded. Any enemies of the French found themselves allied with the British, and Constantinople was happy to defer ratification of the terms of Kléber's surrender to London. The British government, however, rejected the negotiated terms as too lenient.

The French dug in, ruling Egypt for another eighteen months, during which Kléber was assassinated by a Muslim wielding a knife. As a more meaningful deterrent to the populace, his killer was publicly executed according to Islamic law: The hand

*Napoleon and General Kléber upon defeating
the Mamelukes*

with which he had committed the crime was burned off to the elbow, then he was lowered onto a stake for slow death by impalement. (His cremated remains were taken to the National Museum of Natural History in Paris, where twenty-five years later Muhammad Ali's Arab exchange students reported seeing them on view with the mummies.)

In 1801, less than half of Napoleon's original 34,000 troops who had landed in 1798 finally surrendered to an invading force of British and Turks, which included Muhammad Ali as an obscure junior officer of Albanian mercenaries. Legend has it that before he landed on the beach at Abukir, rough seas pitched him into the bay and British soldiers saved him from drowning.

NAPOLEON HAD ORIGINALLY sailed with a combined force of 54,000 men—38,000 soldiers, 16,000 sailors, and 154 savants—and a library of 287 books. Muhammad Ali's later modernization of Egypt began with the printing presses that traveled with Napoleon's campaign, presses for which Napoleon brought Arabic as well as French fonts. At one of Napoleon's banquets in Cairo, each guest found on his cushion, translated into his respective language, companion volumes of the Koran and Thomas Paine's *The Rights of Man*.

Until then, Islam had rejected printed books as

sacrilegious—calligraphy was considered "Queen of
the Arts"—condemning the Arab world, if not to intellectual, certainly to technological stagnation vis-à-vis
the West. Western technological expertise was based
on the accessibility of information. Arabs had named
the stars, but Europe's shared science stole the fire of
their secrets. By the last decade of the eighteenth century, even with all of Europe at war, every sailing ship
made use of the British *Nautical Almanac* of celestial
navigation. While Muslims, wherever they were, prayed
toward Mecca, European ships and explorers synchro-
nized with Greenwich.

There is a symbolic image of the European Enlightenment on the march in Napoleon's habit of
reading while riding at the head of his army, tearing
out the pages of his book as he finished them and
tossing them over his shoulder to be snatched up and
read one by one, soldier by soldier, or out loud in
groups, back through the ranks.

Along with the Grand Army of the Orient, Napoleon brought his *corps des savants*—his "living ency-
clopedia" of 154 scientists and specialists recruited
from l'Institut de France: engineers, mathematicians,
archaeologists, zoologists, mineralogists, physicists,
chemists, economists, Arabists, geographers, cartog-
raphers, astronomers, painters, poets, and even a
musicologist—almost all of whom remained stranded with the army in Egypt.

During those three years, the savants investigated

Savants measuring the Sphinx, drawn by
Dominique-Vivant Denon

everything in and about Egypt—the ancient monuments and the contemporary inhabitants, the feasibility of a canal from the Red Sea to the Mediterranean (abandoned when an engineer mistakenly calculated the former higher than the latter by thirty-three feet), the annual flooding of the Nile, its flora and fauna and especially the mysterious development of baby crocodiles, the phenomenology of the mirage, the medicinal value of mummies (sold by the pound in Europe for centuries, a commodity as profitable as spices). These compiled studies became the monumental *Description of Egypt*, so ambitiously detailed that the first of its eventual twenty-four volumes was not published in Paris until 1809 and its last not until 1828. Almost three hundred artists and printers also participated in this collective master-piece of the Enlightenment. Saint-Hilaire spoke for all when he said of the *Description of Egypt:* "We have gathered the materials of the most beautiful work a nation could undertake. Mourning the fate of so many brave soldiers, who after so many glorious ex-ploits succumbed in Egypt, one is consoled by the existence of a work this precious."

But it was Dominique-Vivant Denon who first brought Egypt back to France. Napoleon's artist-playwright-diplomat-pornographer-documentarian had accompanied the army pursuing Mamelukes up the Nile into Nubia, making his sketches and taking his notes often under fire, often interrupting them to escape with his life. With the phenomenal luck that characterized his entire life, he returned to Cairo just in time to accompany Napoleon back to Paris. Denon's voluminous drawings and exciting popular account of the campaign—with chapter headings such as "Depart for the Unknown"—had a head start of over a year on the more scholarly work of the savants, whose enthusiastic chronicler and press agent he became.

The debacle in Egypt was only military. For the savants, who continued their avid investigating and collecting while marooned with the army, those three years were a triumph and tribute to the human mind. Napoleon's Egyptian adventure became the defining experience, the legendary youth, of a whole generation of French intellectuals. The "Egypto-mania" that they carried back to Europe mytholo-gized into a romantic fascination of the new century—and inspired ten-year-old Jean-François Champollion to start studying the Eastern languages with which he would decipher the hieroglyphs of the Rosetta stone in 1822. Napoleon died the year before that, but his surviving savants celebrated Champollion's success as their general's greatest victory.

3

The Renaissance
Barbarian

UHAMMAD ALI'S long admiration of
the French began when he arrived in
Egypt to fight them early in March of
1801. When the French were at last allowed by the
British to evacuate and sail away in July of 1801, the
resulting power vacuum in Cairo found Muhammad
Ali at the head of his own army. Four bloody years
later, with the vestigial Mamelukes and his other enemies dead or doomed, this minor cutthroat warlord
became Ottoman viceroy of Egypt.

Nominally answerable only to the sultan in Constantinople, Muhammad Ali literally _owned_ Egypt
from 1805 until he died in 1849. From the beginning, he was unique among Muslim rulers in his
enthusiastic openness to Europe. But as with Napoleon, his genius had two faces.

A decade after consolidating his power in Cairo and reinternationalizing the port of Alexandria, he captured Mecca and Medina, ostensibly restoring Islam's holy cities to the "true believers" of the Ottoman Empire while taking all of western Arabia for himself. His dominion eventually extended south to Aden and north through Syria and the entire eastern Mediterranean. His appreciation of sea power, unusual in the Arab world, inspired him to build Islam's first powerful navy. His conquest of Nubia and Sudan in the early 1820s enabled him to monopolize the African slave trade for the next fifty years. At the same time he was graciously and ambitiously courting Europe, France in particular, for the Western expertise with which he modernized Egypt. Under Muhammad Ali, Egypt went from the Stone Age to the Enlightenment in a single personality.

Muhammad Ali was a contradictory force unto himself—an up-from-nothing barbarian who was illiterate until middle age, but who sent the youngest of his seventeen sons (he recognized thirty children as his own) to be educated in Paris and wrote to him there: "You will learn as you grow older and mature that I have performed great deeds out of nothing. As for you, my son, you will attain . . . in the city of light . . . the arts and sciences where learning in all its branches is established, that city where countless great men were reared and which continues to rear others equally great."

Muhammad Ali

Muhammad Ali berated underlings—distinguish-ing a Turk "donkey" from an inferior Egyptian "pig son of a pig"; regularly threatening to have them be-headed, impaled, whipped, buried alive, drowned in the Nile, or to have their beards pulled out hair by hair—but foreign travelers unanimously recorded his exquisite courtesy. Though he was partial to the

French, visitors from everywhere were welcome at his court. Egypt's history may have meant nothing to him, but he astutely used Europe's fascination with his country's past to modernize its future. An American engineer who came to study the Pyramids was flattered to stay and build bridges and dams. An Italian geologist was commissioned to mine niter and manufacture gunpowder. An English entrepreneur, though after antiquities, was sent up the Nile to build a sugar refinery and a rum distillery.

But the greatest of all of Muhammad Ali's national resources may have been the timely allure Egypt held for the French. Some, like Bernardino Drovetti, stayed on in freewheeling careers. After Napoleon was finally defeated at Waterloo in 1815 and his army was disbanded, many of his men returned to Egypt for the jobs Muhammad Ali gave them training his army and navy and organizing his bureaucracy.

It is ironic to see these men who were products, or even dregs, of the eighteenth-century European Enlightenment—the social and scientific humanism that would lead through 200 years of democratic upheaval to the birth of America and the death of the French and Russian monarchies—putting themselves at the disposal of an unencumbered Muslim autocrat.

Among these nineteenth-century Egyptophiles was Frédéric Cailliaud, a watchmaker's son, whose first expedition up the Nile was in 1816 with none other than Bernardino Drovetti. Drovetti was suspicious of the young Frenchman, reluctant to encourage a potential competitor in tomb robbing. But Cailliaud's encyclopedic enthusiasm won Drovetti over, and, upon their return to Cairo, the consul championed him to the viceroy. Within moments of their introduction, informed that Cailliaud's skills included gemology and jewelry design learned from his father, Muhammad Ali appointed him royal mineralogist and sent him off to search for emeralds along the Red Sea. Ancient Greeks had written of emerald mines in Egypt, but the fields were lost for 7,000 years before Cailliaud rediscovered them. The scholarly adventurer returned to Cairo with an initial ten pounds of emeralds for Muhammad Ali, who had no idea what the rough stones were until it was explained to him that they needed to be cut and polished into jewels. Consequently held in great esteem by the viceroy, the scholarly adventurer traveled all over Egypt on official sanction for the next six years.

In the Enlightenment tradition of Napoleon's *corps des savants* two decades before, Cailliaud accompanied the initial Egyptian invasion of Nubia and Sudan in 1821. It took the huge army three days to cross the White Nile south of Tuti Island; thirty men and 150 camels drowned. Cailliaud, commissioned to search for gold, explored 400 miles up the Blue Nile; his sail was the first seen on the river since ancient Egyptians had come south for slaves.

Cailliaud saw giraffes "to right and left" along
the Blue Nile near Sennar, as well as monkeys, hyenas, and elephants whose herds then ranged north
nearly into Egypt. He described "the agile and un-
easy hippopotamuses" that swam bellowing around
his boat. The next three years of Muhammad Ali's
conquest, however, would drive the wild animals out
of the area, so that in 1824 Zarafa was born 200
miles away to the southeast.

At one point in this voyage, while on board, Cailliaud reported hearing along the river "abnormal
noises [that] persisted as we searched closer," whose
source was discovered to be the hatching of crocodile
eggs. While his companions kept nervous lookout for
adult crocodiles, which were known to prey on the
young, Cailliaud went ashore and midwifed the
hatchlings, assisting and studying them, measuring
and recording in lapidary detail how they emerged
unrolling a foot long, more than twice the length of
their eggs, hissing at him. In a gesture typical of both
the curiosity and the saving-nature-from-itself pre-
sumptuousness of the Enlightenment, he took one of
the hatchlings back to the boat and tried unsucces-
fully to raise it.

In the foothills of Ethiopia, the Blue Nile curves
into an unnavigable 400-mile gorge, through which
Cailliaud described the army's difficult progress in a
letter back to Drovetti in Alexandria: "I am the only
voyager who has gone beyond the Kingdom of Sen-

nar and penetrated as far as 10° latitude . . . into a
mountainous country, covered by dense woods, following a torrent that we must cross 8–10 times a
day, without a path, terrified mostly by wild animals
and surrounded by numerous enemies who . . . give
us no rest, attacking at any hour of the day."

ALONG WITH REPUTABLE rogues like Drovetti and
intrepid intellectuals like Cailliaud, Muhammad Ali's
Egypt attracted the on-the-run rabble of Europe. By
far the most colorful and talented of these renegades
was "Colonel" Sèves.

In 1798, at ten years of age, Octave Joseph Anthelme Sèves was so unruly that his parents disowned
him into the French navy as a cabin boy. At seventeen he suffered an ax wound, fighting hand to hand
against the British at Trafalgar. Two years later, after
"a very grave act of indiscipline," Sèves was ca-
shiered from the navy and joined the army, where he
made corporal in his first month. During Napoleon's
second conquest of Austria in 1809, Sèves was captured and held prisoner in Hungary for two years.
Repatriated into the Grand Army of France, he
served with distinction throughout the Napoleonic
Wars, regularly promoted and wounded by gunshot,
saber, and lance. In 1814 Sèves was a lieutenant of
cavalry when he received the cross of the Legion of
Honor.

After the British-led victory at Waterloo ensured restoration of the French monarchy, general amnesty was declared for Napoleon's army and Sèves was discharged as a captain. Legend has it that he then became involved in a plot to free Napoleon's great general Michel Ney from prison. The plot failed, and Sèves escaped to Egypt, where by 1819 he had promoted himself to colonel and Muhammad Ali had hired him to search for coal in the hills between the Upper Nile and Red Sea. Returning to Cairo without success, Sèves found the city celebrating Muhammad

Octave Joseph Anthelme Sèves

Ali's conquest of the holy cities of Mecca and Medina. The viceroy, setting his sights next on Nubia
and Sudan, sent Sèves to Aswân to organize and train
a new army along French lines.

At first the Muslim conscripts despised Sèves as a
foreigner and an infidel. Théodore de Lesseps, whose
younger brother, Ferdinand, would build the Suez
Canal fifty years later, described the trainees aiming
at Sèves during target practice: "Repeatedly he ordered 'Fire!' and heard the bullets whistle around
him." Their aim improved to a point where they
eventually shot his horse out from under him. Sèves
survived and prevailed, though, and it was his trainees who conquered the Upper Nile and escorted the
hunters who captured Zarafa. Tens of thousands of
the slaves taken in Sudan became in turn the army
Sèves and his staff trained to defeat the Greeks in the
spring and summer of 1827, while Zarafa was walking from Marseille to Paris.

EXPLORERS, ENTREPRENEURS, even Christian mis-
sionaries were provided with assistance as Muhammad Ali picked their brains and opened Egypt to the
world. As well as his son and the thousands of other
students he sent to Europe, he dispatched cadres of
Arab intellectuals and specialists to learn Western
ways. And just as the Crusaders returning from the
Holy Land had opened the European mind centuries

earlier, these Muslims took the details, the worldly
aptitude, and the philosophical import of the Enlightenment home to Islamic debate.

In addition to his French military advisers and
officers, the viceroy hired Western educators, scientists, managers, and experts in all fields to create the
administrative and economic infrastructure upon
which, he realized, the military power of a modern
nation depends. He had his bankers and financiers
instructed in Italian, which was then the language of
international commerce. Diplomacy was conducted
in French.

Speaking only Albanian, Greek, and Turkish himself, Muhammad Ali was constantly attended by relay
teams of scribes, who translated his dictation into
Arabic. His chief interpreter with Europeans and
everyone else was his lifelong factotum and alter ego,
an Armenian named Joussouf Boghos, who was the
second most powerful man in Egypt well before the
viceroy appointed him minister of foreign affairs.
Despite his power, Boghos's loyal and selfless humil-
ity made him the only early associate who survived
Muhammad Ali's metamorphosis into a world figure.

Commissioning a French mercenary to Marseille
to oversee construction of three battleships, Boghos
wrote instructions: "While in Europe [you] must
gather all possible information about how things are
done, the new inventions that [you] think adoptable
and useful to Egypt for industry, commerce, manu-

Muhammad Ali

facturing, the sciences, the arts; finally [you] must
further with zeal the intentions of His Highness . . .
for the regeneration and the civilization of the beautiful country he governs.''

Muhammad Ali financed this regeneration and civilization of his beautiful country with ruthless taxation and the most rapacious wholesale slave trade of all time. He augmented his huge army of Sudanese slaves by continuing to conscript Egyptians. The viceroy's European mercenaries were aghast at the misery in the training camps, where the conscripts, "lacking even clothes," died at the rate of twelve to eighteen a day. To escape Muhammad Ali's press-gangs, the practice of mutilating young men—customarily by amputation of their trigger finger—became a village profession, usually of old women. (On the felucca that carried French novelist Gustave Flaubert up the Nile in 1850, eleven of the fourteen crewmen were missing their right forefinger.)

Consistent only in his contradictions, Muhammad Ali could send one of his sons to conquer the Sudan, then rebuke his excessive taxation of the tribes: "It was your duty to gain [their] trust . . . by kindness and just treatment. . . . instead you have alienated them. . . . We are not there for money, but for slaves."

Before Muhammad Ali completed his conquest of the Upper Nile in 1823, 5,000 human captives every year were sent from the slave market at Shendi down the Nile or to the port of Suakin on the Red Sea. While the prolonged massacre of the conquest killed 50,000 natives, 30,000 survivors were taken as slaves. Only an estimated half of them lived to reach

Cairo, where most of those died ill-fed and unused
to the cold and without immunity to the diseases of
civilization.

Over the next half century, though, the viceroy
and his heirs diligently increased the annual trade to
50,000 men, women, and workable children—more
than 2 million people, at least two for every square
mile of the Sudan. Whole tribes died out as villages
were emptied of able-bodied inhabitants, leaving behind only those who were too young or too old or
sick or otherwise physically useless.

Just as he was indifferent to the people he en-
slaved, the Albanian outsider who did not know his
own birthday cared little for the antiquities of Egypt,
which he dismissed and gave away as "ancient debris." Most Egyptians agreed with him. Tomb robbers were at work in pharaonic times, and the
Sphinx lost its nose to Mameluke target practice.
Peasants and their animals inhabited the ancient
temples and tombs, living higher and higher on the
rubble of their ancestors. The monuments were
quarried for their prehewn stone. Mummies littered
the ground, in such profusion that a human bone
came to hand as easily as a stick or stone when an
improvised tool was needed.

Deciphering the hieroglyphs meant nothing to
Muhammad Ali. As far as he was concerned, Egyptology was merely valuable public relations with Europe. Then, in 1828, the year after Zarafa's arrival

caused such a sensation in France, Charles X sent Champollion on his momentous expedition to Egypt. Champollion deplored the vandalism and destruction of the ancient sites and was moved to write to the viceroy. This letter was Champollion's second great contribution to Egyptology, justifying preservation by pointing out to the old mercenary that tourists would make Egypt rich. Champollion's argument, along with the enormous fortunes made by Drovetti and other collectors, convinced Muhammad Ali in 1835 to pass the first law controlling the excavation, trade, and exportation of Egyptian antiquities.

4

Stealing Egypt

LAKE NASSER, created by Egypt's Aswân High Dam, now extends south for nearly 500 miles into Sudan. At its bottom are the original sites of colossal ancient monuments that were dismantled and removed by stonecutters and reassembled on higher ground in the 1970s. Forty-five villages along the Nile were evacuated and submerged, along with the Second Cataract where Zarafa entered Egypt.

Lake Nasser has caused the water table under the Sahara to rise, bringing the desert to life at odd places as far away as Algeria. Along the Nile, though, this fact alone has finally doomed pharaonic Egypt. The higher groundwater leeches salt up into stone that has withstood millennia; the salt bubbles and bursts surface paintings and carvings into flakes, which the wind blows away into dust. Egyptologists estimate that within the next 200 years—the same amount of time since Egyptology started with Napoleon's invasion in 1798—all of ancient Egypt outside of museums will be gone.

The first museums of Egyptology were established in Europe in the excitement that followed the deciphering of the hieroglyphs. Suddenly, Bernardino Drovetti, who had trafficked in antiquities for more than twenty years, found the booty of his grave robbing honored into official collections. He became rich and enjoyed the respectful gratitude of scientists and kings, but it never occurred to him that he was stealing ancient Egypt safe for posterity.

Drovetti was a Piemontese born near Turin. At twenty he had served in his local militia as part of twenty-five-year-old Napoleon's "liberation" of northern Italy from the Austrian Empire of the Hapsburgs. The war wound that crippled Drovetti's writing hand did not dampen his adventurous spirit, and in 1802 he arrived in Alexandria as French vice-consul—a commercial bureaucrat in a backward foreign land, hired by a former army officer under whom he had fought—where he stayed to serve his adopted country and himself with great public honor and private profit. In 1806, the year after Muhammad Ali became viceroy, Drovetti was promoted to consul general (succeeding his boyhood friend, Matthieu de Lesseps, whose son Ferdinand would also hold the post before building the Suez Canal).

Bernardino Drovetti

Although his official tenure was interrupted in 1814 when Napoleon's abdication restored the French monarchy, Drovetti remained in Alexandria, having well established himself in Egypt's international business (and grave robbing) community as an indispensable ally and private adviser to Muhammad Ali. He was reappointed consul general in 1821 and held the post until 1829 with the grand title of "Consul General of His Very Christian Majesty in the Valley of the Nile."

The past was a golden commodity for Drovetti, who dug it up and sold it to wealthy travelers and collectors all over Europe. His official diplomatic position enabled him to moonlight as an entrepreneur of antiquities, thanks to whom no *cabinet de curiosités* need be without its mummy.

The *cabinet de curiosités*—"chamber of curiosities"—was a phenomenon of the Enlightenment, an intellectual fad in which the educated and/or wealthy elite of Europe and America collected whatever struck their fancy. European aristocracy also assembled menageries of exotic animals. Physicians and veterinarians preserved malformed fetuses and other biological monstrosities.

These personal and professional *cabinets de curiosités* and private zoos were serious avocations, with which collectors also entertained and impressed their visitors. Even as pretentious or eccentric folly, this packrat mania was a telling manifestation of an age when truth seemed to be the ultimate and absolute democracy, accessible to any diligent amateur, and science was as simple as preserving a specimen in formaldehyde or flying a kite in a thunderstorm.

The *cabinet de curiosités* evinced the Enlightenment ideal of the mind able to scrutinize anything into a science. And nothing was too small to matter. The slightest thing was a potential clue, a puzzle-piece of the world at large. Some of these personal collections accrued into critical mass—like the ball

Bernardino Drovetti with his agents

of string that grows into a Guinness World Record—
and became official museums.

These collections and menageries developed a
profitable world trade in all manner of exotica, and
Drovetti was at its African forefront. He was also the
Godfather of early Egyptology. As the earliest and
longest-tenured European in Muhammad Ali's
Egypt, Drovetti had built a network extending from
the viceroy himself to the far-flung village headmen
and work gangs and various other "agents and opera-
tives" who made grave robbing risky for his competitors.

And yet, like Muhammad Ali, Drovetti was also a

man of charismatic and even endearing charm—a cultured pirate who rarely traveled because of his chronic seasickness—admired by his colleagues and customers the world over. Cailliaud and Sèves became the most well known of the many foreigners who owed their careers in Egypt to Drovetti, just as others were unsuccessful there without Drovetti's support.

Throughout Drovetti's twenty-seven years in Alexandria, travelers were moved by the generosity of this honorary Frenchman who was such a genius at making himself invaluable. They were touched by the sight of him scrawling his mark with the hand "mutilated," as Chateaubriand wrote, "in the service of his country!" In 1806, soon after Drovetti was named consul general, the celebrated author was sailing home to France from Jerusalem—a new mistress had demanded that he make the pilgrimage in return for her favors—when adverse winds detained his ship in Alexandria for ten days. He found the ancient port "the saddest and most desolate place on earth" and gratefully memorialized an image of Drovetti's life there: "Monsieur Drovetti has erected on the deck of his house a tented aviary, where he raises quail, partridges, and diverse other species of game birds. We passed the hours walking in this aviary, speaking of France."

During his seven-year interlude as a private citizen, Drovetti remained Europe's access to Egypt.

The director of customs in Marseille was a veteran
of Napoleon's Egyptian campaign and indicative of
Drovetti's clients: "Monsieur Cailliaud has told me
that in Upper Egypt one can easily procure mummies of animals and I would be very glad to make a
collection of them, I have yet only a mummy of a
woman, a cat, and a lizard." Soon he was thanking
Drovetti for receipt of a mummified ox and "new
objects each more precious than the others . . . the
mummy of the monkey, the package of snakes and
the morsel of ancient bread."

While purveying mummies and other oddities,
Drovetti formed his three famous collections, amass-
ing and selling one after the other starting in 1824.
He trafficked also in African animals. Among the orders he filled were: a pair of gazelles to Napoleon's
sister, Princess Caroline of Naples—to be received
"in the spring . . . with those of the Empress [Jose-
phine] if bad luck does not intervene . . . male and
female"; ostrich feathers to the French ambassador
in Constantinople—"Madame was very happy with
them"; a "superb horse from Dongola" and "exquisite" coffee and wine to an Italian prince in Turin, as
well as an oryx "received dead" and donated as the
first example of its species to the local public museum of natural history.

Drovetti provided Arabian stallions to Vienna,
Nubian sheep to Moscow, shells and fossils from the
Libyan desert to Paris. The king of Savoy corre-

sponded with Drovetti about obtaining an elephant. An Italian botanist wrote to him, "If ever some botanist presents himself to you and he is able to make you a gift of some Egyptian plants gathered in that country so rich in vegetation, don't forget me." The Russian Imperial Society of Naturalists also inquired, "Would you not have some traveling entomologist who might consent to sell insects?"

In 1822, five years before Zarafa arrived in Paris, Egyptomania suddenly became Egyptology when Jean-François Champollion deciphered the hieroglyphs on the Rosetta stone. Named for the site where Napoleon's troops had discovered it at one of the two mouths of the Nile (the other is Damietta), the Rosetta stone had been surrendered to the British in 1801. Champollion studied wax impressions of it that had been taken back to France. As a schoolboy, he had been inspired by Denon and by the Egyptian artifacts in the *cabinet de curiosités* of his local prefect, Joseph Fourier, the physicist-politician who had been among Napoleon's *corps de savants*.

Champollion's discovery transformed the "excavation" of Egyptian antiquities into serious science and big business. With his very first translation— the cartouche-encircled name of Rameses II— Champollion rewrote Shelley's famous poem, coincidentally about the same pharaoh, "Ozymandias": " 'Look on my works, ye Mighty, and despair' " became " 'Look on my works, ye Mighty, and *BUY!* ' "

Legend has it that this first breakthrough translation so excited Champollion that he ran through the
streets of Paris to tell his brother, "I've got it!" and
fainted. If true, the anecdote sadly foreshadows the
stroke he did not survive only ten years later.

Competitive intrigue delayed full publication of
Champollion's findings until 1824. The year before
that Drovetti had offered his initial collection—the
world's first extensive look at ancient Egypt—for sale
to the king of France, Louis XVIII. The king rejected
it, advised by clerics that the artifacts sacrilegiously
predated the bibilical history of man. So the collection was bought for 400,000 lire by the king of Sardinia, who thus created in Turin the first museum of
Egyptology. Despite making a fortune, Drovetti
shared the disappointment of French Egyptologists
that antiquities of such significance did not go to his
adopted country. After Louis XVIII died in September 1824, Drovetti was further chagrined to learn
that another Egyptian collection—assembled by
Drovetti's British consular counterpart and archrival
in Egypt, Henry Salt—was to be bought by the new
French king and Anglophile, Charles X.

Salt's collection founded the Egyptian Museum
of the Louvre, and Champollion was named its first
curator by royal decree on May 30, 1826—while
Zarafa was halfway down the Nile. That fall Champollion's older brother wrote to Drovetti reporting
Egyptology's "great attraction since my brother's dis-

Jean-François Champollion

covery; governments are forming museums and cre-
ating chairs of Egyptian archaeology . . . in Paris,
Rome, Bologna, Pisa . . . ; there is one incontestable
point. . . . Paris is the veritable center of Egyptian
archeology. There is but one regret, which is that
your beautiful collection was not [our] cornerstone."

Champollion personified the Enlightenment in

training his mind since youth to decipher the hieroglyphs, which he accomplished without first setting
foot in Egypt. As famous as Champollion immediately became, he respectfully hung on Drovetti's
counsel for his long-awaited royal expedition to
Egypt: "I am consulting you alone, Sir, on the opportunity of the journey and when to execute it. You
alone know the country and the facilities or the ob-
stacles well enough. . . . One word from you and I
set off." And during Champollion's expedition along
the Nile—when, after thousands of years, he was the
first and only man able to read the story of ancient
Egypt—his letters to Alexandria exemplify the affection Drovetti inspired generally: "I beg you to tell
Monsieur Drovetti . . . we drank to his health, before
the ruins, two bottles of his excellent wine."

5

A Royal Gift

GREEK CIVILIZATION virtually disappeared after the fall of the Roman Empire and the subsequent barbarian invasions. When the Ottoman Turks conquered the region in the fifteenth century, there was little left of Greece but its language and its monuments. Stimulated by the eighteenth-century Enlightenment and the revolutions it had wrought in America and France, Greek writers, rather than mobs, inspired their country back to life. Their new literary nationalism erupted into the Greek War of Independence in 1821.

In the first years of the Greek Revolution, the sultan sought only limited military assistance from Muhammad Ali, fearful of bringing the huge Egyptian army of Sudanese slaves so close to Constantinople.

That suited the viceroy, as it became clear that the sultan could not win the war without him. The longer the sultan waited, the weaker he would be to deal with Muhammad Ali's own eventual plans for independence.

When the Egyptians were finally ordered to Greece in force in 1824, the Sultan's commander in chief complained that Muhammad Ali's 30,000 arriving troops exceeded the need of the conflict. These troops were commanded by Muhammad Ali's son, whom Sèves accompanied as chief of staff. They commenced operations in March of 1825 and immediately defeated the Greeks, who for their part were led by British mercenaries, in battle after battle.

Needing a replacement for Sèves back in Egypt, the viceroy hired one of Napoleon's former generals, Pierre-François-Xavier Boyer, who took over training and outfitting the continually growing Egyptian army. Boyer was a veteran of Napoleon's Egyptian campaign—an officer of the Grand Army of the Orient that Muhammad Ali had come to fight as a young Albanian mercenary.

Articulating the Enlightenment idealism of those long-ago days, Boyer had declared: "Bonaparte, general of the Republic, will find me always ready to follow him everywhere, but if I suspected that he ever wanted to be a Caesar, I would be the first Brutus to plunge a dagger into his heart." A quarter of a century later, Boyer had become the mercenary—

like so many other former citizens of the lost French republic.

Boyer, a baron of the Napoleonic Empire whose name would later be inscribed as a hero of France on the north side of l'Arc de Triomphe, admired Sèves's success with troops hostile to his training—"The creation of the viceroy's army is owed to the perseverance of this officer"—but he detested the staff Sèves left him: "The species of Europeans that I found as instructors in the ranks . . . are all refugees . . . all the worst rabble on earth, without character, without faith, without law and without honor."

Officially a private citizen, Boyer made indirect reports to ministers of the French government, who sought to dissuade the viceroy from fighting the Greeks. The ministers used Boyer to hint at French support if Muhammad Ali were to switch sides and declare his own war of independence on the Turks. (Fifteen years later, when called upon, that support was not forthcoming.) Drovetti, whether or not he was aware of Boyer's double game, criticized him as "more eager to make money than to accomplish French projects."

Without the backing of Drovetti, whom Boyer acknowledged as the viceroy's most trusted *grand ami,* the ex-general's second career in Egypt also ended badly. After only two years of his ten-year contract, Boyer's resignation was, according to Drovetti, "accepted without difficulty," and he returned to France at the end of September 1826, sailing with his horses aboard the same ship that carried Zarafa from Alexandria to Marseille.

AT THE BEGINNING of the Greek revolt, French newspapers celebrated Turkish losses to "the intrepid patriots, rifle in hand, saber between their teeth." But as the initial Greek victories against the Turks became decisive defeat at the hands of the Egyptians four years later, Muhammad Ali emerged as the villain of Europe.

The French press, presenting the Greek War of Independence as the Enlightenment's ultimate underdog struggle for human rights, clamored for European intervention. There were reports of atrocities committed by the barbarian Arabs upon the defenders of the birthplace of democracy: "It is said that the fury of the Turks is frightful and already . . . more than 2,000 women and children have been massacred." These reports inflamed demands for an equivalent renewal of the Crusades.

In 1824 Charles X assumed the throne of France. Early the next year, after the dramatic Egyptian victories in Greece, the czar of Russia threatened to come to the aid of the insurgents—not to fight for democracy, which he abhorred, but to liberate a Christian country from the Muslims. The British, whose politics of practicality acted only in their national interest, were more concerned with keeping the Russians out of the Mediterranean; to that end, they opposed intervention, but only so long as France also stayed out of the conflict.

Despite French public opinion, the new ultraroyalist king, Charles X (whose own problems with the press would ultimately force his abdication in 1830), had no sympathy whatsoever for democratic uprisings. Three days after mobs had taken the Bastille on July 14, 1789, he had led the first royal exiles out of France. In 1793, the French Revolution had beheaded his oldest brother, Louis XVI, who was a better amateur locksmith than he was a king. A sister had gone to the guillotine in 1794.

Moreover, Charles X was an anomaly in nineteenth-century France: a Frenchman who was beholden to the British, grateful for his undisturbed asylum with them during France's revolutionary and Napoleonic eras. Sailing into Portsmouth in 1795, after the first six wandering years of his exile, the prince of émigrés had found creditors waiting for him on the dock. His Britannic Majesty's government, averting embarrassment to their royal guest (as well as to their own hospitality), had disembarked him by night and saved him from debtors' prison.

With the restoration of the monarchy, the zoo in Paris had once again become the royal menagerie. Soon after Charles X became king, his Ministry of Foreign Affairs circulated a directive from the National Museum of Natural History in Paris to French ambassadors and consuls around the world—"In-

Charles X

structions for Travelers and for Employers in the Colonies"—expressing the new monarch's desire to enrich the royal menagerie with animals from everywhere. Drovetti lost no time in dispatching a gift of two African antelope, male and female, for which he received the new king's gratitude.

Experienced in privately trafficking animals, Drovetti's consulate now became officially involved in sending animals to France as official gifts from Muhammad Ali. The Ministry of Foreign Affairs in Paris had discovered an obscure maritime act empowering consuls in the Middle East to require "the captains and owners of French ships to embark curious foreign animals destined for the royal menagerie. . . . [Seamen] obstinate in their refusal will be made the object of official complaint and will be severely punished."

These animals made life aboard French ships crossing the Mediterranean even more interesting. The archives in Marseille document the arrival from Alexandria of a parrot originally from Yemen along with a feline gift from Muhammad Ali vaguely identified as a "wild cat" in need of a new cage "as soon as possible." The captain of another ship from Alexandria, upon arriving in Marseille, immediately requested a chain to restrain a hyena also about to escape its cage. In the margin of a memo to the captain acknowledging the danger of "this ferocious beast" and requesting assurance of "all necessary precautions . . . in order that the public safety not be compromised in any manner," the local authority emphasized, "without a moment to lose."

Drovetti's eagerness to ingratiate himself with the new king, Charles X, and Muhammad Ali's desire to befriend him, combined to inspire the consul general with the idea of sending France its first giraffe. Such a spectacular and historic gift would insinuate Drovetti further into royal favor and perhaps help lessen resentment toward the viceroy's imminent invasion of Greece.

EVEN BEFORE ZARAFA was born in the fall of 1824, the viceroy had ordered her capture. His edict traveled six days via the recently completed canal from

Alexandria to Cairo, then two months up the Nile to his new slaving garrison at Khartoum. That fall after the rains, Arab hunters set out from Sennar, 200 miles farther south on the Blue Nile. Ten days' march brought them into the savanna highlands of what was then called Ethiopia and is now southeastern Sudan. In December Zarafa was barely two months old, no taller than the men who killed and butchered her mother into enough meat to be carried by four camels.

Of all land animals, giraffes have the largest eyes. Their prodigious eyesight enables them to identify and communicate with one another visually from as far as a mile away, beyond scent or sound, and this trait has allowed them to evolve the aloof dignity of nearly silent creatures. Their resulting "flight distance"—the distance they will allow themselves to be approached by a predator—is just inside 100 yards, farther than any other animal of the savanna. They seem endowed with an uncanny early warning prescience that inspired the ancient Egyptians, in their hieroglyphs, to use the figure of the giraffe to mean "foretell."

The giraffe's curious, unhurried, elegantly awkward gait belies the fact that an adult can one-kick a lion to death and out-accelerate a horse. It was said by Arab hunters that a horse able to run down two giraffes in one day was fit for a king. An adult giraffe can initially outrun a horse, but its lungs are small for its exaggerated body. Like all larger animals of the savanna, the giraffe has evolved more speed than breath. The Arabs would have chased in relays, tiring the mother giraffe, then closed in to hamstring the animal with their long swords before spearing her. Crippled, she would have fought to the death, still able to kill a man with a flailing front hoof or to bring down a horse with a battering swing of her long neck and head.

The markings of every giraffe are unique, like human fingerprints. The mother's hide, one inch thick and impervious to the acacia thorns that sheltered her calf from lions and leopards and packs of hyenas and jackals, would have been sold and cut up for tribal warriors' shields or water buckets or head-to-hock-long straps and whips. Her tail, deemed magical since prehistoric cave paintings first depicted giraffes as being hunted and valued, would have become a royal flyswatter. Some of its wiry strands would have been woven into talismanic bracelets, such as poachers still provide to the African tourist trade today. Her long tibias would have served as bludgeons or been fashioned into flutes. Her meat, considered delicious, would have been sold or bartered.

A second young giraffe, another female in poor health, was also captured. Since giraffes live in loose groups of three or four adults, the females mothering single offspring after a long gestation of fourteen months, these two captives were possibly half sisters. Over the next few days, they were carefully calmed into accepting milk from the hunters. Then both calves were strapped with their hoofs bound aboard camels and, in caravan with the divided remains of their mothers, began their journey north with the march to Sennar.

The two orphaned giraffes had each other for solace, but they survived capture because they were so young and still nursing. The hunters knew from brutal experience that a weaned giraffe, larger and stronger, would either cripple itself fighting to escape or die of self-imposed starvation. Untamable, impossible to keep alive, all but the youngest were killed. More often than not, even the youngest were damaged in their ungainly panic. But if they were small enough to be controlled without harm for a few days, feeding reassured them and transferred their attachment from their mothers to their human keepers.

From the day of her capture through the two and a half years of her journey via camel, Nile felucca, seagoing brigantine, and her own four legs to Paris, Zarafa's survival was aided by her size: She remained petite. She was a Masai, the most subtly marked and smallest of the three subspecies of giraffe; Rothschild's are midsize; Reticulated, with their more sharply defined markings, are by far the largest. Giraffes at birth stand from four to six feet tall, and grow slowly, more or less tripling their height as adults. A male Reticulated can attain eighteen or twenty feet and weigh 3,000 pounds. Zarafa's full height at maturity, though, was just over twelve feet—small even for a Masai—beguilingly miniature and manageable.

As property of the despotic viceroy, these two young giraffes were worth the lives of their keepers. Their own hunger, and gentling hands at mortal risk, kept them alive at first on camel's milk. Later, cows provided the twenty-five gallons each giraffe grew to consume every day.

This early bonding with humans—in, of all places, the slaving hellholes of Sennar and Khartoum—tamed the calves into virtual pets and explains Zarafa's famous affection for the gawking crowds she encountered all her life. Even in Sennar and Khartoum, she was a rarity. In France, unsophisticated provincials and blasé Parisians alike gathered to be frightened or awed or au courant or merely curious to see this novel creature from an alien world. But whatever their expectations, by all accounts everyone who ever saw her was enchanted by her, undeniably because she showed such surprising trust in them.

6

The Sea of Milk

$\mathcal{A}$T SENNAR the two little giraffes were transferred to a felucca and joined the human trag-
edy—the "black ivory"—of slaves riding the
Blue Nile to Khartoum. Unlike the slaves, however,
the calves remained in the new garrison to mature
and strengthen for their journey down the Nile.

The viceroy was delighted by the news from
Khartoum. Having two giraffes, he would be able to
use one to impress his friends the French and the
other to curry favor with the British. Drovetti and
his syce, Hassan, would ensure the advice necessary
to both giraffes' survival. Hassan was a desert Arab
who had given up his nomadic life as a hunter.
Now he was Drovetti's expert animal handler, thanks
to whom France would have its first giraffe and,
masha'Allah, so would Britain.

Muhammad Ali had been through this process once before with Hassan. In 1823, prior to taking charge of Drovetti's mail-order menagerie, Hassan had accompanied another giraffe, a young male sent by Muhammad Ali to the sultan in Constantinople—a gift attesting to the viceroy's expansion of the Ottoman Empire with his conquest that year of Nubia and Sudan. Constantinople had not seen a giraffe since the sixteenth century, when one was sent to the gala celebrating the circumcision of an adolescent heir to the sultanate. Muhammad Ali had looked forward to the sultan's gratitude. Hassan knew from hunting and capturing giraffes that the animal required its continued regimen of milk. But the Turkish fools in charge had ignored the uncouth desert Arab, and the viceroy's spectacular tribute to himself had died.

This time, Hassan's instructions, conveyed personally to Muhammad Ali by Drovetti, would have had the force of royal commands issued steadily from the palace in Alexandria to functionaries in Cairo and on up the Nile to those responsible for Zarafa and her companion. Hassan would be heeded from afar while the calves were raised in Khartoum, or heads would roll.

⌒

THE GARRISON at Khartoum had been established only months before the giraffes arrived. During their sixteen months growing up there, the military camp expanded into a village of mud huts housing the overseers of Muhammad Ali's new slave trade.

At Khartoum in spring and fall, migrating storks fill the sky—huge flocks of pairs mated for life, flying so slowly it seems impossible that they remain airborne—following the Nile to and from their nests in Europe. As the stork flies, Alexandria is a thousand miles from Khartoum, the same distance the S of the Nile travels just to reach the Egyptian border.

From Khartoum the various chronologies of the giraffes' journey down the Nile are confusing. The later French reports were based on roughly translated conversations with Zarafa's four Arab handlers in Marseille, two of whom were anonymous, not even appearing in the records until they returned to Egypt soon after arriving in France.

The other two men were officially identified by Marseillaise customs records as having sailed with the giraffe from Alexandria and conducting her later to Paris: Zarafa's chief handler, Hassan, and his assistant, Atir.

Drovetti described Atir as "my negro servant," but Saint-Hilaire introduced him to the king of France as Drovetti's former slave. In Egypt at the time, it was customary for expatriate Europeans to buy servants, who, by virtue of their residence with foreigners, were then considered free. Slaves became employees, especially among the French living in

Egypt. In 1794 the Revolution had outlawed slavery in France and its colonies, and had granted Negroes all rights of French citizenship. The egalitarian leveling of French society had also initially banned membership in clubs, business and religious organizations, and even literary societies.

Atir was Sudanese, identified by his tribal facial scars as coming from south of Sennar. It is tantalizing and so wishfully romantic to infer that he could have raised Zarafa in Khartoum and, with or without Hassan, brought her down the Nile before their life together in Paris. But the Arabs' sketchy, secondhand account of the giraffe's capture and subsequent journey argues that neither man joined her sooner than Cairo.

With Drovetti's nephew translating between the Arabs and the scientists in Marseille, the facts of Zarafa's voyage from Khartoum to Alexandria are scattered in marvelous linguistic mumbo-jumbo. Hand-fed milk by humans since her infancy, she remained unweaned as a young adult. The Arabs explained her preference for milk over water with the existence in her native country

> of a large lake, the water of which is white, sweet and slightly warm, and it is there . . . even from far away, that [giraffes] are accustomed to come to drink. This is why [in captivity] they want only milk [fresh from camel or cow], which has the

> *color, taste and temperature of the water of this*
> *white lake . . . [which] is very long, but not very*
> *wide [and where] one finds a great number of*
> *crocodiles and gross animals which, according to*
> *their description, must be hippopotamuses. . . .*
> *The Arabs name the lake in question El Baar*
> *Habiat, which means, according to Mr. Drovetti,*
> *"the sea of milk."*

Searching maps for this lake, the French scientists found El Baar Abial, which is the Arabic appellation of the White Nile. Zarafa, though, was captured farther east and arrived at Khartoum via the Blue Nile.

Most confusing of all are the *seize lunes,* the sixteen months the Arabs reported—or so they were translated—as the amount of time between Zarafa's departure from Sennar until her release from customs in Marseille on November 14, 1826.

The wonderful account of Zarafa compiled by one of the academicians in Marseille, a man identified only as Mr. Salze, states: "Accompanied by another of the same sex and age . . . This young giraffe made the journey from Sennar to Cairo, part way marching with caravans, part way on the Nile in a barge that had been prepared especially for her."

Before the Turks pacified the Upper Nile, the point of embarkation on the river would have been at Aswân, northern terminus of the desert crossing, just past the last of the six Cataracts downriver from Khartoum and safe from the marauding tribes. But

Geoffroy Saint-Hilaire, writing thirdhand the next spring while en route with Zarafa from Marseille to Paris, confuses matters even further: "These giraffes journeyed, at first on foot with a caravan from Sennar to Asyût . . . then on the Nile, from Asyût to Cairo."

Asyût is 250 easily navigable miles downriver from Aswân, an unnecessary journey by land. But given nineteenth-century Europe's limited knowledge of the Nile—and of the viceroy's recent conquest of Nubia and Sudan—it would have been a logical mistake to assume that if Zarafa and her companion had to travel overland past the six Cataracts, such a journey ended at Asyût. Asyût was the head of the famous ancient caravan trail the Darb al-Arba'een—"the Road of Forty Days." This trail, however, did not follow the Nile; it angled northeast out of western Sudan, last leg of the long route from Timbuktu, and Zarafa's entourage would never have used it.

Then there is the heat. If one counts those sixteen months backward from Zarafa's November arrival in Marseille, it seems impossible that two eight-month-old giraffes—for whom none other than the redoubtable viceroy himself had commanded utmost precaution—would be marched across the Sahara in mid-July. The waterless march from Berber to Aswân took over two weeks of grueling thirty-mile days, and desert temperatures in July ranged from freezing at night toward 140° Fahrenheit during the day.

Also, this illogical chronology—subtracting the

four months between Zarafa's arrival in Alexandria and the day she set foot on the French mainland—requires that her journey from Sennar down the Nile lasted an incredible eleven months. By contrast, in 1849 a hippopotamus bound for England sailed from Khartoum to the Mediterranean in just sixty days.

There is also the matter of the other giraffe's health. Zarafa's companion's legs, too crippled to stand soon after she arrived the next year in London, were incapable of carrying her very far. Seeing both giraffes in Alexandria, Drovetti reported to his minister of foreign affairs that the companion was "sickly and will not live long" while Zarafa was "solid and vigorous." Neither giraffe was full grown, but surely both were too large to have been packed on camels as they were when captured as calves.

And most significant, both giraffes were still unweaned, each consuming by this time up to twenty-five daily gallons of, according to the later report of Hassan and Atir in Marseille, cows' milk. A reliable supply of this amount of milk while en route from Khartoum to Cairo would have required a contingent of at least six cows, animals that could not have survived marching with the caravans.

HISTORICAL COINCIDENCE and seasonal logic argue that Zarafa and her companion, via two voyages sixteen months apart, were shipped the entire 2,000

Feluccas on the Nile

miles down the Blue Nile and the Nile from Sennar
to Alexandria.

The larger feluccas of the Nile were as long as
forty feet, with crews of more than a dozen men.
The boats were tillered from the roof of an aft cabin,
which ranged in size from a simple poop to an upper
deck half the length of the hull. Two elegantly
exaggerated triangular sails forward, lateen-rigged—
suspended from long yards atop shorter masts—
could be seesawed and pivoted, overlapping aloft or
spread wide to either side. The keel was broad and
shallow to skim over the shifting river bottom, lower
in the bow to facilitate muscling it clear when the
boat often ran aground. High aft, the feluccas were
levered and hauled and poled backward over the

rocks of the six Cataracts between Khartoum and
Aswân.

Except in the dangerous torrential floods of summer, or at winter's ebb when the current was too
low to help pull the feluccas over the Cataracts, the
Upper Nile was easy sailing. May and June were the
ideal time of year, when the river started to rise with
the wind from the south. From Khartoum past the
Cataracts and on to the sea was a voyage of two
months—which fits the July arrival of the giraffes in
Alexandria.

The giraffes would have ridden on deck, amid-
ships between cabin and masts, in the shade of a
canvas tent open fore and aft to the breeze. North-
bound feluccas also carried monkeys loose on deck,
climbing the masts and riding in the rigging as depicted thousands of years ago in ancient Egyptian
wall paintings and bas-reliefs. At each Cataract, the
giraffes would have been off-loaded while the monkeys stayed aboard, adding their screeeches to the
hauling songs of the men at the ropes on both banks
and poling from the deck.

When Zarafa traveled down the Nile in that
spring of 1826, by far the majority of passengers on
the river were slaves bound for Cairo. The human
captives must have wondered at the sight of another
felucca carrying two giraffes. What might the Ethiopian women have thought, crowded together in despair, seeing these creatures from their homeland?

At night the feluccas beached side by side and the
crews congregated. Flaubert described one such encounter: "The master . . . presents us with bunches
of ostrich plumes. . . . One woman is having her hair
combed with a porcupine quill: the thin braids are
undone one by one and then rebraided. . . . On all
these boats, among the women, there are old ne-
gresses who make and remake the trip continually;

Ancient wall painting of the giraffe at Thebes

they are there to console the new slaves and keep up
their spirits; they teach them to resign themselves to
their fate and they act as interpreters between them
and the trader, an Arab."

As Zarafa and her companion sailed past Thebes,
which is now Luxor, there were two other giraffes
already there—both of them up in the hills on the
western bank, both of them also royal tribute, both
of them older than the obelisks at Luxor Temple, and
both waiting several more decades to be discovered
by Egyptologists.

One of these is carved on the tomb of the first
woman to rule Egypt, Hatshepsut, whose expedition
to the land of Punt in the fifteenth century B.C. not
only records the first anthropological interest in another culture but also brought this giraffe back to her
menagerie that is history's earliest known zoo.

The other giraffe at Thebes was painted 3,500
years ago in the tomb of the vizier Rekhmire. One of
the vizier's duties was to receive foreign tribute on
behalf of the pharaoh, and here among the menagerie on Rekhmire's walls—along with a little bear
and a baby elephant from Syria and an African leopard, all tamed to a leash—is a giraffe with a green
monkey playfully climbing its neck. Like Zarafa, this
giraffe is young, barely taller than the two Nubians
who are responsible for it, docile enough to be led
by ropes tied only to its forelegs.

7

Farewells

NORTH OF CAIRO, still 100 miles from the sea, the Nile divides to complete its journey. The two main branches separate and, with their tributaries, fan out across the delta like the umbel of a vast papyrus. Mediterranean-bound feluccas took the western branch to the Mahmudiyya Canal, down which they continued for five or six more days, quartering toward the setting sun to the port of Alexandria.

For its first 700 years, Alexandria was the most international and learned city on earth. After Alexander the Great conquered Egypt in 332 B.C., his new namesake capital developed into the main Mediterranean port between Europe and Asia. Under Alexander's successors, the Ptolemies, Alexandria became the architectural rival of Athens and Rome. Their lighthouse was one of the Seven Wonders of the World. They created a mythic library, for which all arriving ships surrendered any reading material to be copied by scribes. Ancient Alexandria was a city of 300,000 people and 700,000 books.

The last of the Ptolemies was Cleopatra, who lost Egypt to the Romans in the first century B.C. After she and Marc Antony committed suicide, their two sons, the youngest of whom was six, were taken to Rome as hostages. The victorious Octavian, Julius Caesar's adopted son, ordered the execution of eighteen-year-old Caesarion, Cleopatra's son by Caesar.

The Roman invaders burned the library, but Alexandria remained the commercial and intellectual center of the Mediterranean world for another three centuries. The Romans dug the first canal from the Nile to Alexandria, and Egypt became the granary of their empire; the population of the city grew to 1 million, second only to Rome.

The commerce and culture of three ancient civilizations—Egyptian, Greek, Roman—thus met and flourished at Alexandria. Ptolemaic cartography and astronomy situated Alexandria at the very center of the universe. But with the decline of the Roman Empire, this city at the crossroads of heaven and earth and history degenerated into a decadent backwater of political intrigue, insurrection, famine, and disease. At the end of the fourth century, when Christianity became the official religion of the Roman Empire, Alexandria's ancient temples were razed and its institutes of learning were closed. In the seventh century, the Muslim conquest completed the city's destruction. The famous lighthouse was toppled either by an earthquake or, according to legend, by Arabs looking for buried gold. The ancient Roman canal was left to fill with silt as the Muslims abandoned Alexandria and founded their new capital at Cairo.

Napoleon's invasion reestablished Alexandria's strategic importance. Muhammad Ali revitalized the port with Egypt's foreign trade, which became so important to him that in 1819—after he had the canal redug and named for the Turkish sultan, Mahmud— Alexandria became his primary residence. He had grown up in a tiny Macedonian harbor town, the son of a soldier who also chartered ships and traded in tobacco. The sea was more familiar to him than the desert, and Alexandria was a more luxurious and worldly reminder than Cairo of how far he had come.

AT ALEXANDRIA the sea is ever changing—turquoise shallows and purple depths and vast outer blue that turns dark green when the wind roughens it too choppy to reflect the sky, silver gray under clouds and patched with golden columns of sunlight— constant only in its immensity and, after the snaking current of the Nile, violently alive. Incoming swells explode into rainbows against the limestone fortress of the Mamelukes at the entrance to the harbor. The light, too, is mercurial, moody without the solid heat of the desert. Arabic sounds different here, and faces change as Egypt turns Greek.

After the overwhelming fact of the Nile—where the heat and the landscape and fifty centuries of history confirm the irrelevance of any particular life—Alexandria is a physical and emotional relief, a beautiful and confusing letdown. Body and eyes no longer suffer, and the mind no longer searches in awe for the shelter of a detail—momentary shade, a drink, some small living touch like the green monkey climbing that other Zarafa's neck 3,500 years ago.

The magnificent ordeal of a journey down the Nile is over, but Alexandria is strangely melancholy. Time passes here on the human scale, fleeting and never exactly recurring. Depending on the light, the foursquare Mameluke fortress between mild harbor and wild ocean changes from tawny to glaring white, a sand castle only five centuries old. Instead of the desert mirage that taunts with its vision of Muslim paradise, rainbows disappear here with the breathing rhythm of the sea. The traveler from the south is reluctant to proceed, homesick for immortal things.

THE TWO GIRAFFES arrived at Alexandria early in the summer of 1826. Seeing that Zarafa was so much healthier than her companion, Salt wanted her.

Drovetti's correspondence reports that the viceroy
settled the matter by having the rival consuls draw
lots for the animals. Or so the story goes. Given
Drovetti's nature and his favored relationship with
Muhammad Ali, it is unlikely that the French luck of
the draw was left to chance. Omitting details, Drovetti wrote to his minister of foreign affairs in Paris:
"I am happy to inform Your Excellency that the out-
come was favorable to us. Our giraffe is solid and
vigorous, the one that went to the King of England
is sickly and will not live long."

Two thousand miles from where they were born,
the giraffes spent their last three months together
on the grounds of Muhammad Ali's palace overlooking the Mediterranean. By the end of September,
Drovetti had organized Zarafa's transport from Alexandria and her reception in Marseille.

Rather than invoke his consular power to com-
mandeer passage for her on a French ship, he en-
trusted her to a fellow Italian, Stefano Manara,
captain of a Sardinian brigantine named *I Due Fratelli*. After twenty-four years of doing business in the
port of Alexandria, Drovetti well knew the various
European vessels and their captains; it made more
sense to take expensive precautions than to ship "the
beautiful animal of the king" as resented cargo.

Passage for Zarafa and her party on *I Due Fratelli*
cost the treasury of France 4,500 francs, close to
750 American dollars of the time. The enormity of

this expense, and of the official commitment it represented, can be seen in the fact that it was well
over twice the total amount incurred during Zarafa's
seven months with her growing entourage in their
specially constructed stable in Marseille.

Hassan was now in charge of Zarafa, assisted by
Atir. Her new entourage comprised three milk cows
and a brace of antelope Drovetti was sending along
as "a new gift offered to the sovereign by the consul
himself." The hold also contained two horses that
belonged to General Boyer, who was returning to
France from his abbreviated military service to the
viceroy.

Drovetti considered sailing with Zarafa to Marseille, but his chronic seasickness kept him from
going. Although his seasickness was well-known, he
may have also used it as an excuse; for by not making
the voyage, he could not be implicated in the failure
of the enterprise if the giraffe died en route. In his
stead, Drovetti sent his nephew along to translate for
the indispensable Hassan.

A hole was cut in the deck of the brigantine to
allow Zarafa to stand upright below. The edge of the
hole was padded with straw to cushion impact to her
neck in rolling seas. A canvas canopy was erected to
protect her from sun and rain. Separated for the first
time in her life from her companion, Zarafa was
shipped standing among the animals in the hold
while her neck and head rode up with the humans
on deck—a sad farewell but an elegantly defining

image, symbolic of the fact that, though her size and strength made her formidable, she was much more the honored pet than a wild or even domesticated animal.

I Due Fratelli sailed from Alexandria with Zarafa and her little arkload of new companions on September 29, 1826. The brigantine identified Zarafa's royal significance by flying the flags of both Egypt and France. Drovetti bid his adieus in Italian to his nephew and Captain Manara, in French to Boyer, in Arabic to Hassan and Atir. Boyer's staff, seeing him off with military honors, added pageantry to the departure.

Drovetti's nephew carried a letter full of concerned instructions from the consul to the agent of foreign affairs in Marseille:

> *I beg you also to make sure that the Giraffe be provided in quarantine with everything necessary to her keep, and placed in accommodations of an appropriate temperature. Although this quadruped is not as sensitive to cold as would be supposed from the latitude of its native land, I think it will be necessary to leave her in Marseille until the spring.*
>
> *. . . If the cows that I am putting onboard to provide milk for the Giraffe no longer give enough after their arrival, I would be grateful if you would be willing to advise your person in charge of this provision to procure additional of it to the amount of 20–25 liters per day. The*

continuation of the use of milk is indispensable. A Giraffe, sent three years ago to the Sultan in Constantinople, perished because they ceased to give it this drink in the spirit of economy.

. . . I take the liberty on this same occasion of commanding into your good care two antelope, which I am sending to the King and which I have announced to the Minister of the Royal Household. The male is affected with a malady that . . . seems to be centered internally . . . presumably not scabies, for this would have already been communicated to the female.

. . . I am writing His Excellency the Minister of the Royal Household to take [Atir] my negro servant (one of the guardians offered to care for the animals) as far as Paris, and even to keep him with the Giraffe if she judges him apropos; this animal could prove difficult to habituate to a European handler.

ZARAFA'S CRIPPLED COMPANION remained in Alexandria until the following January, then her voyage to Britain was interrupted at Malta for six months. She arrived in London in August of 1827 and, in contrast with Zarafa's spectacular reception in France six weeks earlier, was caricatured in cartoons hostile to King George IV. Deteriorating, soon unable to stand, she was rigged into a hanging harness

The giraffe sent to England

to support her weight off her legs. A cartoon of the
king and his mistress hoisting the giraffe in this con-
traption was captioned: "I suppose we'll also have to
pay to have her stuffed." The giraffe died in London
in August 1829. Omitted in the cartoons, but around
her neck in serious portraits, is the amulet contain-
ing verses of the Koran—her *hijab* against the evil
eye—identical to the one worn by Zarafa.

8

Camelopard

~~~

THE SAILING ROUTE from Alexandria to
the Mediterranean ports of Italy and France
lay northwest to Crete and west along that
island's southern coast to its end, then northwest
again to the Sicilian port of Messina. Near the end
of the second week out, weather permitting, ships
steered dead ahead for Sicily's Mt. Etna rising from
below the horizon. *I Due Fratelli* had clear sailing
and would have seen the volcano's long wind-driven
plume of smoke from 125 miles away, a day and
night before arriving off the sickle-shaped peninisula
of Messina's small harbor.

Just three miles across the strait from the kicking
toe of the Italian mainland, Messina was the historical
center of Mediterranean maritime traffic—founded
by ancient Greek colonists, taken by Carthage, imperial Roman gateway to Alexandria and Constantinople

and the Eastern Empire, Byzantine center of learning, court of Norman warrior-poets and birthplace of the sonnet, and periodically destroyed over the centuries by cataclysmic earthquakes.

In Zarafa's time, Messina was on the way to everywhere, European port of entry and exit for Africa and Asia. Ships from all three continents lay to here in the narrow roads to rest and take on fresh water and provisions. Because of the plague, which since the fourteenth century had killed an estimated one-third of the total world population, crews and passengers were required to remain on board in quarantine.

It was here, off Messina, from the deck of *I Due Fratelli*, that Zarafa and Hassan and Atir had their first sights and sounds and tastes of this other world. Vendors plied the anchorage in small boats supplying fruit and vegetables and regional delicacies and wine to travelers confined to their ships. The coins of payment were collected in pots filled with vinegar and other disinfectants.

At Messina, the tropics meet Europe. Fertilized by centuries of volcanic ash from Mt. Etna, palm trees mingle with evergreen oaks and pines. In fall and winter the public squares and private gardens keep their jumbled profusions of green, while bare trees line the more European boulevards. From the port, the rugged hills behind the city—intricately terraced with orchards of olives and citrus and minuscule vineyards—hide the sight of winter snow

on Etna, which is known locally as Mongibello, "beautiful mountain." (Even so, at 11,000 feet, it is Europe's highest and deadliest active volcano; since the ancient Greeks gave it a name meaning "I burn" 2,800 years ago, it has erupted more than 135 times, the single worst eruption killing 20,000 people.)

The autumn sun of Messina is strong, still closer to Africa than to France and the European continent; but the wet season that has ended in Africa now begins here, chilling the longer nights and bringing a northern, rainwashed sparkle to the light.

The young Arab intellectual Rif'â-at-Tahtâwî

made the voyage from Alexandria to Marseille six months before Zarafa. Tahtâwî also was sent to Paris by Muhammad Ali; sailing with him were the fifty-three other members of the viceroy's first scholarly mission to Europe. The Arabs traveled aboard a French brigantine called *la Truite*, and their fellow passengers included the parrot from Yemen and the wild cat in its disintegrating cage.

Tahtâwî described Messina as he saw it from the ship he was not allowed to leave: "We stayed five days in its port. From afar we saw its high palaces, its lofty and sublime temples. At twilight we saw the lighting of its lanterns and its torches, which were still shining after sunrise. I think a festival took place while we were there, for we heard carillons. The melody executed by those bells was so harmonious!"

At that time, Zarafa and her companion were still hearing the call to prayer in Khartoum, one month before they embarked together down the Nile to their different lives. Tahtâwî went on: "On the soul's emotion at the sound of the carillon when the bell-ringer is skillful and a man enjoys it for the first time, I recited the eloquence of a poet: 'Hardly had he arrived, ringing a bell, when I asked him, "Who taught the gazelle about the playing of the bells?" And I interrogated my soul: "What are the blows that are moving you to grief? Evaluate this! Is it the striking of the bells or the wound of separation?" ' "

WHAT MUST THE MESSINESI have thought of Zarafa, of this long-necked creature whose body was out of sight below deck? In the passionate way Italians have of taking their history so personally, they would have reported that this camelopard—neck and face of a camel, spots of a leopard—was not the first to be seen in Messina. Julius Caesar had brought Europe's first one back from Cleopatra's Egypt in 46 B.C.

To have survived its transport, that giraffe, like Zarafa, would have been captured young enough to tame for its initiating journey down the Nile. In Rome, it accompanied Caesar's triumphal procession of hundreds of caged lions and leopards and black panthers and other strange and dangerous beasts, baboons and green monkeys, hunting salukis (the world's oldest breed of domesticated dog), Nile parrots and parakeets, flamingos and ostriches, slaves and ivory and emeralds and gold, and "a great number of elephants bearing torches"—all the wondrous spoils of African conquest that history would come to know too well.

Soon after, in the games celebrating the dedication of Caesar's Forum, he made a gift of this giraffe to his fellow countrymen and treated them to the spectacle of having it killed by lions. To indicate the fabulous pomp of Caesar's return to Rome, Pliny the Younger reported that 400 lions were also sacrificed at those opening games of the Forum. The later Roman historian Dion Cassius suspected that "generally people exaggerate these things . . . but I am going to speak of the camelopard because it was then the first to appear in Rome."

In the centuries after Caesar, hundreds of giraffes were imported to Rome for killing sport, either in private hunting menageries or most often in the arenas of the Circus Maximus and later the Colosseum (opening day of which was reputed to have turned the new sand red with the slaughter of 5,000 animals, mostly lions and bears).

Such spectacles originated around 275 B.C. when Roman legions returned from their conquest of Pyrrhus, the King of Epirus, with 142 elephants, the first exotic animal captives of the expanding empire. Rome had never seen elephants before, but they were notoriously feared for having routed its soldiers at Tarentum, one of two battles so devastating even to the victorious Pyrrhus that they are the source of the term *Pyrrhic victory*. To avenge this humiliation, the Roman Senate sentenced the elephants to death en masse before the entire population of the city. The fear and inexperience of the executioners, who kept their distance with arrows and javelins, made a long gory business of it.

By the time of the Christians, three centuries later, these gruesome celebrations of imperial conquest had evolved into public and private amusement. At the drunken banquets of Emperor Heliogabalus, guests were invited to throw live pheasants to his lions. The festivities continued as revelers who passed out would wake to the same fate, finding themselves locked in a room with a lion or a leopard or a bear. Several hungover victims, not sharing the emperor's sense of humor, died only of fright.

Caesar himself incurred huge personal debt entertaining Rome with public Games of Animals, which came to be expected as the civic duty of any citizen celebrating a triumph, military or civilian. Caligula, who was a contemporary of Christ and became emperor shortly after the Crucifixion, effected a cost-saving symbiosis between menagerie and penal system by feeding criminals to his lions.

As masters of far-flung disparate lands, the Romans indulged their fascination with mortal combat between animals that would never encounter each other in the wild. The arena crowds loved the comic relief of lions scrambling like oversized house cats after rabbits and parakeets whose wings had been clipped. A giraffe would find itself pitted against a bear from Asia or a fighting bull from Iberia or, very often, against the emperor. Gordian I counted 100 giraffes among his public kills. From what we know of Zarafa and her upbringing, none of these or any of the other giraffes since Caesar's could have arrived alive in Rome as other than a tamed and trusting pet.

After the Roman Empire fell into the Dark Ages, 1,000 years passed before the next and last giraffe appeared in Europe. The Crusades against Islam had reinternationalized the West when, in 1486, the Mameluke sultan of Egypt, Quait Bey, sent a young female giraffe to Lorenzo de' Medici in Florence— "to entertain good relations with the Christians." Lorenzo the Magnificent requited the gift with a bear as white as Quait Bey's limestone fortress then abuilding and still shattering the sea into rainbows at the entrance to Alexandria's harbor.

Saint-Hilaire recounted that Lorenzo's giraffe "was associated, sentimentally at least, with the second stories of the noble houses of the city . . . [to the windows of which] she went every day to take food from the hands of the ladies of Florence, of whom she became the adopted daughter; these repasts consisted of several kinds of fruit, principally apples."

She is memorialized in paintings and frescoes as the first Renaissance depiction of a giraffe from life. One of the seventeen neighborhoods of nearby Siena remains named for her—Contrada della Giraffa. Its riding team and their racing silks commemorate her when they are one of the ten teams from the Contrade selected to compete in the annual running of the horse race called the Palio.

IN 1546 the French naturalist and traveler Pierre Belon saw captive giraffes in Egypt and brought back Europe's first scientific description of them: "It never fails that great rulers, no matter how cruel, love to be presented with beasts from foreign lands. We saw several of these in the royal castle of Cairo, where they had been brought from far and wide: among them is the one [that the Arabs] commonly name Zurnapa. Anciently called Camelopardalis by the Latins . . . she . . . is a very beautiful beast and of the sweetest nature there could be . . . and friendlier than any other wild animal." This is the earliest appearance in print of the Arabic word *zerafa* (mistaken by Belon as "Zurnapa"), which evolved through Moorish Spanish and Italian and French into *giraffe*. Arabic and Greek/Latin abide together today—East meeting West—in the scientific classification of the species, *Giraffa camelopardalis*.

9

Across Sleeping
Marseille

◦~~~

*I*F IT HAPPENS, Sir," wrote the minister of
foreign affairs in Paris, Baron Damas, to his
agent in Marseille on October 10, 1826, "that
another delivery of the same nature (as that of the
lion sent to the King by the emperor of Morocco)
is again addressed directly to you, you will consign
it immediately to the [local Marseillaise] Superior
Administrative Authority: my department will continue to pay expenses that take place outside the
country; but it is the business of the Minister of the
Interior to oversee those incurred in France, and
henceforth you will not have to occupy yourself with
them."

This directive from the minister was sent from
Paris and received in Marseille while Zarafa was at
sea. It does not specifically mention the king's gi-

raffe; but as Drovetti's superior, Damas was well aware that she was expensively en route from Egypt.

After Africa and the missing puzzle-pieces of Zarafa's journey down the Nile, the archives in Marseille and Lyon and Paris bless her to life in wondrous letters, memos, invoices, and contemporary newspapers. It is a stunning revelation—as though something moves out from among acacia leaves and there she really is. And with her emerge the humans in her story, fascinating characters whose official squabbles and mutual concern for her are documented down to the centime.

In the previous century, in just two years, the plague had killed 50,000 of Marseille's 90,000 inhabitants. The epidemic was so swift and devastating that Marseille became known as "the dead city." As a result, the port maintained a rigorous and effective quarantine, expanded in Zarafa's time to deal with yellow fever, which had spread from South America to Spain. Ships were required to anchor between the isles of Pomèques and Ratoneau and If three miles off the mainland.

The new quarantine harbor was called Dieudonnée ("Godgiven") in honor of Charles X's grandson, who was so named because he was born seven months after his father, the duc de Berri, was assassinated. Upon arrival there, passengers were either detained in the medical facility on Ratoneau—the Sanitary Complex of Marseille—or debarked into dinghies and transferred to the mainland quarantine facility, the lazaretto, outside the city.

In May 1826, six months before Zarafa arrived at Marseille, Tahtâwî's large official party—"54 Turkish passengers, among whom are 40 young people destined to receive their education in Paris"—all left the wild cat and the parrot from Yemen on board *la Truite* and commenced their eighteen days of quarantine in the lazaretto.

Tahtâwî described the lazaretto at Marseille as "vast":

> The precinct comprises palace, gardens and solid buildings. It is there that we learned of the quality of the edifices of this country. They are carefully constructed and provided with very numerous parks, fountains, etc. The first day, almost without us even noticing, things happened to us, strange for the most part. For example, we were brought several French servants whose language we did not know and provided with nearly a hundred chairs to seat us, for the inhabitants of this country find it astonishing that a man sits . . . on the ground. Then for the meal . . . the servants placed the chairs around the table, one chair for each person. Then . . . [the food] is distributed to everyone, giving to each on his [individual] plate something that he must first cut with the knife in front of him and that he carries to his mouth with the fork and not

with the fingers, for a person never eats with the
fingers, and never uses either the fork, the knife, or
the glass of another. They claim it is healthier and
more polite.

Animals and their handlers, however, remained
aboard ships while paperwork went back and forth
establishing who would be responsible for their expenses while in quarantine. And now that the foreign
minister had definitively refused to pay for anything
once it set paw or claw or hoof inside France, even
the king's giraffe—especially the king's giraffe—was
forced to await clarification. The customs officials, in
communiqués of florid bureaucratic gentility, were
still dunning the prefect of Marseille, Count Villeneuve-Bargemont, for the two months of three daily
pounds of raw meat and other itemizations for the
wild cat, unpaid by the Paris zoo since June.

(The vague identification of this "wild cat" gives
a good glimpse of how new these animals were to
Europeans. A gift from the viceroy of Egypt, it was
also described as an "African tiger"; and it was the
foreign minister's "lion from the emperor of Morocco." Even Saint-Hilaire and the other zoologists
waiting for it in Paris had to guess at feeding instructions to the prefect: ". . . If the animal is no bigger
than a domestic cat, one pound [1/2 kilo] a day will
suffice. If it is the size of a fox, it will be necessary
to allow two pounds; and if it is the size of a wolf, it

should not be necessary to go beyond three or four pounds.'')

I DUE FRATELLI arrived off Marseille after twenty-five days at sea on Monday, October 23, 1826; but it was not until Friday the twenty-seventh that all eight "servants of the public health" signed their letter to the prefect: "We have the honor to inform you that Captain Manara, arrived from Alexandria, has on board a Giraffe and diverse other animals destined for the royal menagerie. As they are going to be debarked without delay into quarantine, [and seeing] that their sojourn in this establishment will give rise to expenses of feeding and others that [the local agent of foreign affairs] is not at all in charge of paying, we come to beg you to tell us if you authorize us to advance these expenses, as we did on a similar occasion."

The prefect, though, had already been advised of the giraffe's arrival by the local agent of foreign affairs. This man had signed off on the matter by sending along with his memo copies of both Drovetti's letter of "observations" crucial to her survival and the foreign minister's directive refusing to pay her expenses.

Count Villeneuve-Bargemont, the first of the two great heroes of Zarafa's life in France—who became so attached to her that he spoke of her to Saint-

Hilaire as "our adopted daughter"—did not deign to mention money when he wrote back to the servants of the public health. Drovetti's concern became the prefect's matter-of-fact instructions, closing with: "In the case of the least accident to these animals, I ask you to inform me. For their care, a groom and a negro servant of the Consul-General of France have been employed. It is important that they continue to look after them."

IN AUTUMN the chalk isles of the Sanitary Complex change from stark to bleak as the constant wind turns cold. The last wildflowers, flecks of summer, disappear. Stunted clumps of wild rosemary remain clinging to the jagged cliffs and the gravel slopes. Colonies of seagulls hunker amid patches of *astragal*, the minute leaves of which grow along a stem that is an ankle-piercing thorn. The gulls threaten but retreat if approached, not wanting to take flight.

The tiniest of this archipelago, the isle of If, is the site of one of the most famous prisons in and out of fiction. Three hundred years before Zarafa and Hassan and Atir did their bureaucratic time anchored near it, le Chateau d'If was built by Francis I as a fortress outpost to defend Marseille. The young king had seen the isle in 1516, on his way home from conquering the kingdom of Milan. To honor him, the Marseillaise staged a mock naval battle in

Le Chateau d'If

which the ships traded salvos of oranges. Paul de
Lalet described the festivities: "The king got carried
away and took part in this combat that was for him,
like all combat, a party. He laughed throwing . . .
and he laughed receiving full in the chest the ripe
oranges, the golden projectiles that burst upon his
silk doublet starring it with rosy wounds."

    While Francis I was in Marseille, a ship lay at
anchor off the isles with an Indian rhinoceros on
board, en route as a gift from the king of Portugal to
the pope in Rome. This rhinoceros was already well
traveled, having sailed the previous year to Lisbon
from the Portuguese colony of Goa on the south-
western coast of India. It was the first rhinoceros
seen in Europe in 1,000 years, since the games of
the ancient Romans. A Portuguese artist sent a drawing of it to a friend in Germany, who in turn showed
the drawing to the eminent Albrecht Dürer, whose

secondhand elaboration of the creature is now in the British Museum. In Lisbon the Portuguese king tried to pit the rhinoceros against an elephant—both animals, like Zarafa, would have been captured young enough to be tamed and raised as pets—but the elephant panicked at the sight of the rhino and escaped, crashing through the gates of the arena.

At Marseille the rhinoceros was off-loaded to satisfy the curiosity of Francis I—according to legend, on the isle of If where the king later built the squat walled fortress that became the prison. Sailing on toward Italy, the rhino's ship went down in a storm in the Gulf of Genoa, and the unfortunate but commemorated animal was presumed sunk until its carcass washed up on the Ligurian coast. Recovered, it was eviscerated and stuffed with straw and continued on its journey to the Vatican.

The count of Monte Cristo aside, the oddest prisoner of le Chateau d'If was the corpse of General Jean-Baptiste Kléber, who had been left in command when Napoleon abandoned the army in Egypt. After Kléber was assassinated in Cairo in July 1800, his body waited more than a year to be returned to France with the troops. At Marseille, while his assassin's remains proceeded to the natural history museum in Paris, Kléber's coffin was debarked for transfer to his hometown of Strasbourg. But owing to the enmity between the general and Napoleon (exacerbated on Napoleon's part by the fact that Kléber was very much taller), the coffin was detained in le Chateau d'If and all but forgotten for seventeen years.

~

TUESDAY, OCTOBER 31, 1826, marks the day a giraffe first set foot in France. Fishermen were hired and their boat engaged, and, one by one, Zarafa and the two antelope and the three milk cows and General Boyer's two horses were transferred from *I Due Fratelli* to the lazaretto outside Marseille. The invoice for the operation includes rental of the boat for two days, along with costs of a needle, thread, measuring tape, and "forty-eight lengths of checked cloth, to make three blankets, one for the Giraffe and two for the Antelopes."

Other invoices record that, in contrast to Tahtâwî's posh quarantine, Hassan and Atir were given a candle, lighting oil, firewood, and were fed for fifteen days. One of the milk cows had "lost its milk" during the voyage, so augmentation, as per Drovetti's emphatic request, was arranged to fulfill Zarafa's daily need. Hay was provided, straw spread. A mason and his laborer plastered. A guard was set.

Meanwhile, the prefect took the initiative and, even before apprising the minister of the interior in Paris, ordered immediate construction of a stable for the animals on the grounds of his mansion. In his long, detailed letter to the minister seeking "instructions as soon as possible," in which he also requests that the Paris zoo be reminded of its unpaid debt for the wild cat, the prefect finally brings up his own financial need in a P.S. that typifies the man's conscientious enthusiasm:

> *You can assure the administrators of the zoo of the special cares that I am giving to the preservation of this precious animal; I have already assured myself of a site that is fairly green and has good or even free exposure to the midday; I am building there a vast shed of planks that we will heat by means of straw matting against the severity of the season. This construction will necessitate expenses and it is necessary to provide for the animal and for the cows accompanying and nourishing her; the keepers must also have their daily means. Various advances will be made . . . and at every economy possible, but it is essential that . . . you allow me funds.*

And he adds in a second P.S.: "The nephew of Mr. Drovetti just reported that the quarantine facility is very well suited for the preservation of the animals."

On November 10, the prefect received notification from the servants of the public health, in handwriting as ornate as the wording: "Thinking that it would be agreeable to you to know the day of the exit from the lazaretto of the Giraffe and other animals destined for the Royal Menagerie, we have the honor to inform you that they will be cleared in the course of tomorrow, Saturday, the 11th."

The prefect's "vast shed" was not yet completed, however, so Zarafa and the antelope had to wait in the lazaretto, wearing their matching checked blankets, until the following Tuesday. By then the size of the shed, as well as the haste of its construction, had inspired rumors of a gigantic dangerous creature about to arrive in the city.

To spare Zarafa from being frightened by the inevitable mob, the prefect ordered the milk cows and the antelope transferred out of the lazaretto during the day without her. On November 14, 1826, the exotic bovines were conducted through the streets, and as the crowd followed them to the grounds of the prefecture, the ailing antelope put on a satisfyingly fierce display. The parade ended and the crowd dispersed, entertained and relieved. The early dark of autumn fell by five o'clock.

Later that night, between ten and eleven o'clock, Zarafa left the lazaretto with Hassan and Atir and a mounted escort unidentified in the records but presumably a detachment of gendarmes. The horses were skittish of the giraffe, but she calmly fell in behind one of them as Hassan and Atir led her "across sleeping Marseille."

The streetlamps overhead and the echoing cobbles underfoot were new to her. At a narrow passage where the horse preceded her out of sight, she sud-

denly stopped, refusing to move in any direction
until the horse reappeared. Mr. Salze, of the scientific Academy of Marseille, described what happened:

> *As soon as the Giraffe again saw the horse of
> which she had lost sight, she was tranquil, and
> walked following behind it very closely, as well as
> the Arabs who held her by four ropes; but the
> horse was uneasy, its rider had difficulty restrain-
> ing it, and it could not tolerate that the Giraffe
> came from time to time to sniff its rump. She had
> to cross several public avenues, and always she
> tried to reach the branches of the trees near her
> passing, without ever losing sight of the horse
> that she had chosen as guide, and that she fol-
> lowed faithfully to the stable that was her destina-
> tion.*
>
> *One can say that the Giraffe has nothing
> elegant or graceful in the detail of her forms; her
> short body, her high and close-together legs, the
> excessive length of her neck, the declivity of her
> back, her badly rounded rump, and her long and
> bare tail, all these things contrast in a shocking
> manner; she seems badly built, unbalanced on
> her feet, and yet one is seized by astonishment at
> the sight of her, and one finds her beautiful with-
> out being able to say why.*

10

Soirées à la Girafe

A T THE TIME of Zarafa's arrival, Europe had
not seen a living giraffe in nearly 350 years.
The National Museum of Natural History in
Paris had earlier received the hide of a giraffe, packed
in salt and so deteriorated that the scientists could
not figure out how to assemble the specimen. In an
age of curiosity, when everything was new and briefly
amazing—when, thanks to naive science and post-
Napoleonic peace, sophisticated Europe engrossed
itself with wonder after wonder in what seems now
like a collective second childhood—Zarafa was a
major excitement.

She was ensconced in the winterized quarters
built specially for her, the treasured guest of the prefect and his wife (for whom the parrot accompanying
the wild cat had been a gift from Drovetti's vice-

consul in Cairo). The two "tall" antelope were also stabled here in the green and sunny spot selected by the prefect himself on the grounds of his mansion. So were the milk cows, four of them now that one of the Egyptian cows had lost its milk. A partition separated Zarafa from two robust horses. Designed according to Drovetti's recommendation against stoves and stovepipes, the stable was brightly lighted by two windows and a large glass door and required only the aggregated body heat of the animals to warm it.

A cowherd did the milking. The cows were provided with collars and leashes so that they could be tethered on the grounds of the prefecture and, later when the weather warmed, walked to lead the giraffe out into the countryside. Zarafa also had a new collar and two new "large double-long" lead ropes with which Hassan and Atir could supervise her promenades; until her life alone with Atir in Paris, she was walked by a team of at least four and as many as six handlers.

Hassan and Atir, "the two Egyptians," would winter with the animals in the stable. The prefect had ordered their things transferred from the lazaretto along with the hay and grain remaining after fifteen days in quarantine. Military cots and bedding had been requisitioned from the local garrison for them (and, briefly, for the two other anonymous Arabs who are never mentioned in the lazaretto rec-

ords and identified only later in scattered references
to "two of the four" who "accompanied the animals" and soon "returned to their country"). The
men were given two new lamps and lighting oil.
While in Marseille Hassan and Atir would receive
"daily means," which included their food, billed at
46.50 francs per month. In Marseille and en route
to Paris, they were also paid monthly wages—"to
the Arab conductor, 30 francs; to the Negro his aide,
20 francs." The cowherd was paid the same wages
as Hassan, roughly equivalent to five contemporary
American dollars a month.

Mr. Salze and his scientific colleagues from the
Academy of Marseille immediately set to work studying "our young giraffe" from head to feces. Drovetti's nephew served as translator in their interviews
with Hassan and Atir. The prefect received the final
invoices for the maintenance of Zarafa and her entourage in the lazaretto, in triplicate, with a cover
letter that ended: "On this occasion we will take the
liberty to remind you that we have still not at all
been paid the expenses occasioned by . . . the wild
cat."

Four days after assuming custody of Zarafa, the
prefect reported to the minister of the interior in
Paris:

*The Giraffe is most beautiful and commenced very
well in the lazaretto to regain her original vigor*

*that the voyage across the sea had somewhat di-
minished. . . . It is a female Giraffe. Her height
to the top of her head is eleven and one-quarter
feet [Salze soon pinpointed her height, measured
from the ground with a pole, at eleven feet, six
inches]. . . . The most painstaking measures are
being taken for [her] preservation . . . which
under my eyes I am able to supervise myself at
every instant and I was able to economize the
enormous expenses of placing [her and the other
animals] elsewhere.*

Contemporary reports of Zarafa called her "the
Beautiful Egyptian," "the Beautiful African," "the
Child of the Tropics," and all of Marseille was eager
to see her. At first the prefect limited access to her
while Salze and the scientists compiled their observations: "She loves very much to leave her stable, and
when she is walked in the garden of the Prefecture
on days of good weather, it often happens that she
bounds like a young horse. . . . Sometimes she wants
to launch herself into a gallop, dragging along with
her the four Arabs who restrain her, and we have seen
her in a moment of gaiety drag five strong men."

On November 28, 1826, the "professors-administrators" of the National Museum of Natural History in Paris, of which the royal menagerie was part,
wrote in effusive gratitude and curiosity to the prefect:

*The animal that the Pasha of Egypt is sending to
the King is one of the happiest acquisitions that
we have been able to make—never has a living
Giraffe arrived in France, and for eighteen centuries civilized Europe has not seen one [unlike
their colleague Saint-Hilaire, the authors of this
letter were unaware of the giraffe sent to Florence
in the fifteenth century]. . . . We have no information at all on the state of this precious animal;
we do not know if it is young or adult, large or
small, feeble or in good health, wild or tame,
etc., etc. We beg you to have word written to us
on these various points; and in the event that
[the giraffe] should threaten to perish, have a
drawing in color made of it that will tell us exactly its proportions and the forms of its head
viewed from the front and in profile. This will be
with the skeleton and the hide, a slight compen-
sation for us if we have the misfortune to lose [the
giraffe] before its arrival here.*

That winter was unusually severe in the south of
France. The two antelope suffered in their confine-
ment; the male was intractable and dangerous even
to the female; the female became obese.

But Zarafa flourished. A few days before Christ-
mas, Salze completed his sixteen-page "Observations
on the Girafe," in which he reported that she was
healthy, gay, vigorous, and absolutely silent.

*This animal has a very gentle disposition, and
has never been seen to manifest the slightest anger
or malice. She distinguishes the Arab who usually
feeds her, but she does not have an unusual affection for him. She allows herself to be approached by all who come to see her; she does not
like to be touched, and it is only when she fears
something or is bothered too much that she de-
fends herself by kicking forward, whether with
front or hind legs. She never tries to deal a blow
with her head or her horns; on the contrary, one
sees her hold her head very high when one dis-
turbs her or when she is afraid. She often licks
the face, the hands and the clothes of the Arab
who cares for her. Sometimes she licks strangers,
and readily sniffs the persons who approach her.
She appears fearful, heedful of noise: however, she
is not at all frightened by the presence of a great
number of people who approach very close to her.
[She was shy, though, about drinking her milk
in front of strangers.]*

The giraffe's amalgamation of such contradictory
anatomy caused Salze to muse upon her as a kind of
zoological oxymoron, and he wondered whether she
and her species were merely an extraordinary freak
of nature. Zarafa's affection for humans compounded her mystery. Her friendly but unrequited
interest in other animals—horses were afraid of her;

the milk cows she followed everywhere were indifferent to her—conveyed the poignancy of her exile.

By then the prefect and his wife had commenced
to entertain small selective dinner parties—*soirées à
la Girafe*—the highlight of which would be the moment when their grand guests would bundle up
against the cold and the rain and the mistral and be
conducted by lanterns through the gardens to the
stable for their audience with Zarafa.

Imagine the tableaux of disparate worlds (and
odors) meeting there in that shadowy light: traveling
dignitaries and local *nouveau riche* bourgeois and
aristocrats whose families had more or less survived
the Revolution and Napoleon, the women rustling in
silk and in the redolent warmth uncovering their
finery, all paying their privileged respects to the diva
giraffe with her cantankerous antelope familiars, her
milk cows and her Arabs, the Bedouin Hassan and
black Atir in *jalabiyyas* and turbans. Each soirée was
a vivid living *cabinet de curiosités*.

And while the Europeans marveled at the giraffe,
the Muslims marveled at the uncovered women. Tahtâwî could not believe his eyes and fairly gulped at
the immodesty of the women of Marseille: "The
women of this country have the custom of revealing
their face, their head, their bosom and that which
follows below, their neck and that which follows
below, and their arms, nearly to the shoulders. Shopping is in principle the domain of women, but men

have jobs. Thus, the stores, the cafés and that which animated them [at midday] offered us an interesting spectacle."

Such was the extraordinary effect of Zarafa that Salze concluded his scientific "Observations on the Giraffe" as a man enamored of a woman: "It is indeed remarkable that after having contemplated her attentively, one nevertheless keeps only an uncertain memory of her forms and carriage; it is, I believe, this that causes people in general to love to see her often, and each time she gives rise to some new observations."

In a P.S. Salze added that Zarafa had grown an inch and a half taller in those thirty-five days since leaving the lazaretto.

FIVE DAYS INTO the new year of 1827, the prefect reported that "the Giraffe is in the most satisfying condition" while sending his first invoice of expenses to the professors-administrators of the National Museum of Natural History. Savvy bureaucrat that he was, he included the detailed observations and drawing of Zarafa executed "with great zeal" by Salze.

Broaching the subject of the future "translation of the animals" to Paris, he advised against the long Atlantic voyage via Gibraltar and around Spain to the northern port of Le Havre, certain that it was too hazardous to end as happily as the giraffe's crossing

from Alexandria had. Neither did he think she could
travel north by land, not only because of the physical
demands such a trek would make on her but also
because "too many accidents and obstructions could
result from her encountering [traffic of carriages on
the roads] and crowds of the curious." He recom-
mended shipping the animals by boat up the Rhône.

In their response the professors-administrators
did not discuss the prefect's suggestions, but they
were gratefully enchanted by Salze's work and its effect on the minister of interior, under whose financial authority they operated: "This memoir full of
curious details, ingenious perceptions and new observations seeming to us worthy of holding the Minister's attention, we were eager also to show him
the accompanying drawing that gives an idea of the
singular proportions of the animal. We beg you, Sir,
to receive our special thanks for this communication,
but we can not close without expressing again to you
all our gratitude for all that you have so kindly done
and propose to do in this matter for the interests of
science and the museum."

Like Drovetti and the prefect and Salze, the minister of the interior had become another of Zarafa's
conquests, and her expenses were no longer a
problem.

By late February, Zarafa's daily promenade had
become a public event. At noon, when weather per-
mitted, the gates of the prefecture opened and cow-

herds brought the milk cows out on their leashes. The giraffe, encircled by her six handlers, followed wherever the cows led. As the days warmed, their walks lengthened to an hour outside the city and back. On March 3, after her constitutional had been disrupted by "crowds of the curious who do not always permit the maintenance of good order," the prefect wrote to the chief of police requesting henceforth an escort of two gendarmes.

Carriage drivers along the route were warned in advance of the giraffe, and there was only a single mishap when teams panicked at the sight of her. A mule was injured, and two carriages were damaged—which the prefect did not mention to officials in Paris until finalizing accounts in June, when he decided with his characteristic finesse that reparations, though unobligated because the drivers had been warned of the giraffe ahead, should be paid so that "no one is left hostile to [her] handlers."

Later in March the prefect reported to the professors that "we have lost the female antelope. . . . Not one care was neglected and I have seen to preservation of the animal's hide and skeleton." The veterinarian's autopsy declared that she had died on March 4 of violent butting and goring by the male antelope, obesity, and gastritis—a combination of causes "more than sufficient to have occasioned the death."

With spring approaching, letters between the

professors and the prefect and Drovetti were preoc-
cupied with how to transport Zarafa to Paris. There
were no trains yet in France (not until 1837, when
the first line from Paris went less than twenty miles
west to St.-Germain-en-Laye). France had over
30,000 miles of roads that were the best in Europe.
But Drovetti, whose nephew had just returned to
Alexandria and delivered the prefect's request for advice, rejected "the voyage by land" as too dangerous
for the giraffe and for those in charge of her. The
Rhône was too wild a river, and he thought it better
to ship the animals by sea to Le Havre.

On March 15 the professors in Paris wrote to
the prefect reiterating their gratitude and the great
importance of the giraffe to science and to the zoo
and to the minister of the interior and "above all the
interest that we know the King personally puts in the
preservation of this precious animal"—but effectively throwing their hands up and asking, "How do
we get a giraffe from Marseille to Paris?" "Perhaps it
would be a good idea to send from here an intelligent
person capable of directing the operation."

The letter from the professors went on to tell the
prefect about the proprietor of an itinerant menagerie then in Marseille, a man named Polito, who had
witnessed Zarafa on her daily constitutional and had
written to offer them his services in transporting her
by land to Paris. The professors suspected that Polito
was primarily interested in the money he could make

charging people to view the giraffe en route—
"which would not be at all suitable for an object
belonging so directly to the King"—but they asked
the prefect to interview the man in detail and at least
take advantage of his experience in this "genre of
travel."

It took several days for carriages to carry passengers and mail between Paris and Marseille. On March
19, before receiving the professors' letter, the prefect
coincidentally wrote explaining to them why he was
now convinced that a land journey was the best solu-
tion to the problem of getting Zarafa to Paris:

> The Giraffe is always full of vigor and since it is
> no longer cold she is conducted every day some
> distance from the city. It is acknowledged that
> this exercise is necessary to her. It is assured on
> these promenades, for which six men have the
> responsibility of controlling her by the precaution-
> ary means of as many long ropes, that this ani-
> mal easily allows herself to be walked. Her
> companions the cows precede her and she obeys
> in their direction. Neither the noise, nor the traf-
> fic of carriages, nor the crowd of curious who press
> around her cause her the slightest offense. The
> animals who encounter her are no longer fright-
> ened. All of these observations bring to mind the
> possibility of bringing her to Paris by small daily
> journeys. No other manner of transport seems

*preferable to me. River travel, which I first fan-
cied, would present drawbacks combined with
many difficulties; for it is not without some danger of fracture that this animal [is loaded and
unloaded]. . . . I would want you indeed to send
a person from Paris whose analogous knowledge
and aptitude would inspire all confidence and
whom you will charge with the care of overseeing
the transport of the Giraffe, [and for whom] it
would be a good idea to come and study the
habits of the Giraffe before setting out with her.*

A week later, on March 26, the prefect wrote
again to dismiss Polito's proposition, which he
agreed had been "made with a view to speculate on
the public curiosity." And he reiterated: "Everything
convinces me that this animal will be able to go [to
Paris] by small daily journeys, but it is indispensable
that you send an intelligent person capable of directing all things, and who would have to come here
soon enough to see to the arrangements of the departure [and] to take cognizance of the habits of the
Giraffe."

Happier Every Day

VILLENEUVE-BARGEMONT had not been informed that the "intelligent person" coming from Paris would be so eminent as Étienne Geoffroy Saint-Hilaire, one of the premier savants of nineteenth-century Europe.

Delicate and even feeble as a child, and a dreamer after heroes, Saint-Hilaire had given up his ecclesiastic studies when he discovered science. His father allowed him to go to Paris at eighteen and study medicine, on the condition that he also study law for a proper career. Paris and science so inspired him that he completed the law course in less than a year, became a lawyer, and never practiced. His precocious intellectual journey had taken him from theology through law and medicine to zoology when, in June 1793, two months after his twenty-first

Étienne Geoffroy Saint-Hilaire

birthday, he was the youngest of the twelve elected founding professors of the National Museum of Natural History.

The French Revolution created the museum out of the medical school of Paris, originally the royal medicinal garden, le Jardin du Roi. Renamed le Jardin des Plantes, it became part of a new museum intended as an Enlightenment institution of research and teaching—"one of the scientific lighthouses of Europe"—as Georges-Louis Leclerc Buffon, a director of le Jardin, had wished. Young Saint-Hilaire held the title of "Chairman of the Department of Quadrupeds, Cetaceans, Birds, Reptiles, and Fish." His zoology was primarily collecting and dissecting, formaldehyde and bones—until a remarkable moment of history created the world's first municipal zoo. Saint-Hilaire's son, also a zoologist, described it in his biography of his father:

> *After the 10th of August [1792, when mobs attacked the Tuileries palace,] the menagerie of the [later guillotined] King at Versailles was pillaged: a beautiful dromedary, several small quadrupeds, [and] a great number of birds were either eaten or delivered up to the flayer. Only five animals, among them an Indian rhinoceros and a lion, escaped the massacre. But they had, like the others, the misfortune to belong to the King and [so were considered] souvenirs of tyranny. They were besides useless, had to be fed, dangerous to the city. Their death was decided, and the Minister of Finances offered their skeletons to le Jardin des Plantes.*
>
> *Bernardin de Saint-Pierre, appointed steward [of le Jardin] by one of Louis XVI's last acts, refused and denounced the Convention's death sentence against the animals of Versailles as a high crime against science. He demanded that they be transported to le Jardin des Plantes, to become there the nucleus of a menagerie, necessary, he said, to the dignity of the nation, to the study of nature [and] of the liberal arts. . . . The*

*cause of the animals was won; their lives were
saved.*

The menagerie at Versailles was pillaged in August 1792, but the fate of the surviving animals was
not resolved until well after Louis XVI was beheaded
late in January 1793. Saint-Hilaire's nascent zoology
department, which had neither facilities nor person-
nel nor any funds for animals, suddenly owned a lion
and a rhinoceros and their three reprieved companions. There was also a dog that had been raised with
the lion and shared its cage. (Tahtâwî recounted the
nineteenth-century legend that the curious friend-
ship had begun when the lion suffered a painful
wound, which the dog had eased and cured by lick-
ing through the bars of the lion's cage.)

Five months after the museum was founded, on
November 4, Saint-Hilaire was summoned from his
office to receive the unexpected delivery by police of
a white bear and a panther and other animals seized
from a traveling circus. More animals arrived in
turn—another white bear and a mandrill, then a
tiger, two eagles—as the Paris police extended democracy even to beasts by confiscating private menageries. Two other traveling circuses then in Paris
were shut down, and their animals were delivered to
Saint-Hilaire. The animals of street entertainers,
such as dancing bears and trained monkeys, were
also "liberated" from their exploitation.

The museum was mandated as a national institution, and Saint-Hilaire was under no obligation to comply with these seizures by municipal police. But he accepted every animal, improvising their care, ranging their cages around the courtyard of the museum into a public *cabinet de curiosités.* Thus, the zoo of Paris began with nothing but what Saint-Hilaire's admiring son, writing sixty years later, described as his father's "happy temerity to undertake this work of the future, and the happiness of inciting his colleagues to concur."

The Revolution indemnified owners for the confiscation of their living property. Some of these people, dispossessed and unemployed, stayed with their animals and became the zoo's first keepers.

Five years later, at twenty-six, Saint-Hilaire was among the *corps des savants* who accompanied Napoleon to Egypt. He was recruited by his mentors, Claude-Louis Berthollet and Gaspard Monge, who were both nearly twice his age: "Come! We are your colleagues and Bonaparte is our general." Napoleon was not quite three years older than Saint-Hilaire. One day in Cairo, inspecting the Mocattam quarries of the Pyramids with Saint-Hilaire and Monge, Napoleon was moved to grieve that he had not devoted his life to science. Saint-Hilaire never forgot Napoleon saying to Monge: "I found myself a conqueror in Europe like Alexander; it had been more to my liking to march in the footsteps of Newton."

As for so many others of his generation, Saint-Hilaire's three years stranded with the army in

Egypt were a youthful paradise of exotic research and camaraderie. "Happier every day" was his son's description of Saint-Hilaire in Egypt. He studied the crocodiles of the Nile, and this work became a major contribution to the future *Description of Egypt*. He was fascinated by the Egyptian snake charmers, "whose profession is as old as their civilization itself." And he experienced his own biblical miracle in Egypt when, afflicted by the endemic ophthalmia that commonly blinded the native population, his sight returned after twenty-nine hours.

When the French finally surrendered in 1801, the savants faced confiscation by the British of all their assiduous collections. The savants refused to relinquish them. With Saint-Hilaire as their spokesman, they let it be known to their military authority that they would accompany their collections to England as prisoners.

General Abdallah Menou had replaced Kléber in command of the French forces. Menou was the laughingstock of his army, an ex-aristocrat who had converted to Islam and changed his name (*Abdallah* means "slave of God") in order to marry an Arab woman whose family he had presumed was wealthy; but after the wedding her father turned out to be the owner of a bathhouse. Menou's officers were openly scornful of him, and he even had Boyer arrested for insubordination.

Menou claimed the Rosetta stone as his personal

property; but he had no respect for the work of the savants and advised the British commander, General J. H. Hutchinson: "I have just been informed that several among our collectors wish to follow their seeds, minerals, birds, butterflies or reptiles wherever you choose to ship their crates. I do not know if they wish to have themselves stuffed for the purpose, but I can assure you that if the idea should appeal to them, I shall not prevent them."

As a boy of eleven, Saint-Hilaire had been introduced by his grandmother to Plutarch's *Lives of Famous Men*, and this book of heroes had deeply impressed him. At age twenty-nine in Egypt, the man who had saved lions and whole forests full of the French aristocracy's private hunting menageries declared to Hutchinson: "Without us this material is a dead language that neither you nor your scientists can understand. . . . Sooner than permit this iniquitous and vandalous spoliation, we will destroy our property, we will scatter it amid the Libyan sands or throw it into the sea. We shall burn our riches ourselves. It is celebrity you are aiming for. Very well, you can count on the long memory of history: You also will have burnt a library in Alexandria."

Hutchinson allowed the savants to return home with their collections, one of which belonged to Joseph Fourier, the physicist-politician who would later inspire another boy, Champollion, toward deciphering the hieroglyphs. Menou graciously surrendered the Rosetta stone, which was taken to London and remains to this day in the British Museum.

WHILE SAILING TO EGYPT, Saint-Hilaire had become fascinated with the symbiosis of sharks and pilot fish. He found another example of symbiosis along the Nile in the birds that clean the gaping teeth of crocodiles. This reciprocity of wholly disparate species—a predator serving and served by easy prey—had intrigued him ever since the museum's first lion had arrived from Versailles sharing its cage with the dog. When the dog sickened and died, the first replacement introduced into the cage was so terrified that the lion killed it—fulfilling the fate that the dog's expectation seemed to call upon itself—with one swipe of a paw. Eventually, however, the lion accepted a braver canine cage mate.

In that revolutionary era, it seemed that animals, even ferocious animals, also enjoyed a kind of free choice. Saint-Hilaire's colleague at the museum, Jean-Baptiste-Pierre-Antoine de Monet Lamarck (who named both the science of *biologie* and le Jardin des Plantes), formulated the new theory of evolution, which was typical of the Enlightenment in its initial optimism—that acquired characteristics can be inherited (a weight lifter's children could be stronger; the ancestors of the giraffe had stretched their necks reaching to browse). Almost fifty years would pass

before Darwin corrected Lamarck's theory of po-
tentially unlimited possibilities—*transformisme*—into
adaptive survival of the fittest.

In 1830, the year before twenty-two-year-old
Darwin sailed aboard *The Beagle*, Saint-Hilaire de-
fended Lamarck's mutability of species against another famous colleague at the museum, Georges-
Léopold-Chrétien Cuvier, who attributed any and all
genetic change to God. Although Goethe called the
debate between Saint-Hilaire and Cuvier the most
important event in European history, it was not an
out-and-out theological argument. Saint-Hilaire's
studies grew out of, and were not a reaction to, his
ecclesiastical background. Enlightenment science,
with its humanitarian impulse toward improvement,
was not yet a crisis of faith. The intellectuals of the
early nineteenth century were asking God questions,
and He was still speaking to them. (When *The Beagle*
set sail on December 27, 1831, Darwin's mandate
as ship's naturalist was to find proof of the Creation
according to the Bible. By 1845, the year Zarafa
died, Darwin was terrified by the theological implica-
tions of his still-secret theory and confided that it
was "like confessing to murder.")

Another aspect of the Enlightenment research
partnership with God was Saint-Hilaire's interest in
genetic exaggerations—either as successful species,
such as crocodiles, or as individual mutant aberrations. (One of his many monographs on "monstrous

fetuses" dealt with Siamese twins resulting from "the pretended coupling of a dog and a sheep.") Saint-Hilaire was the founder of the science of teratology, believing that the monstrous elucidated development of the normal. So-called freaks of nature were studied and no longer dismissed as oddities of fate.

Almost three decades after Egypt, these themes of Saint-Hilaire's research—reciprocity between species and aberrations of nature—unexpectedly came together in his adventure with Zarafa. She was an anomaly in every way, a bizarre and powerful wild animal serenely attached to humans. He was an eminent fifty-five-year-old scientist, an illustrious intellectual suffering from gout and rheumatism, the most unlikely of all her heroes.

⟨⟨⟨

BY THE END OF APRIL 1827, spring was well along in the south of France. Villeneuve-Bargemont, eagerly expecting Saint-Hilaire, was disappointed that he had not yet arrived. With his customary diplomatic optimism, the prefect counseled the professors at the museum that, while the weather in the north would warm well in advance of Zarafa's small daily journeys, it was also advisable to begin the trip before the great heat of summer came to the south.

The prefect assured the professors, "The state of this Giraffe is always the best. The current [warm] temperature and the green of the fields cause her to

display the most amiable vivacity on her daily promenades. The continuation of the care of which she is
the object seems to promise us that you at the menagerie of the Museum are assured of a precious ac-
quisition."

While waiting for Saint-Hilaire, the prefect happily accepted on his behalf the additional responsibil-
ity of two mouflon—wild sheep with wide curving
horns, indigenous to the mountains of Corsica and
Sardinia—a gift from a local marquis who happened
also to be the prefect's cousin.

En route to Marseille, Saint-Hilaire had stopped
in Montpellier—which he described as "the second
capital of science"—where he negotiated at difficult
length for a "precious collection" of fish brought
back fifty years before by scientists exploring the
South Seas with Captain Cook. The museum in Paris
had long and unsuccessfully tried to obtain the collection. The academicians in Montpellier had always
declined to part with it until Saint-Hilaire, "anticipating the mortification of another refusal," appeared in person to cajole each professor separately
and so persuasively that they were later astonished to
find that they had all agreed to give it to him. While
there, he was honored with a scientific conference to
discuss his latest publication.

Saint-Hilaire arrived in Marseille on May 4,
1827. After the prefect's painstaking care of Zarafa,
he was surprised and happy that the government had

sent such an illustrious scientist to oversee her journey to Paris. The two men became warm friends, and in their subsequent letters they sound like uncles sharing their affection for the giraffe.

Saint-Hilaire spent his first three days in Marseille "studying the appearances and habits of this gigantic animal," accompanying her daily promenades, apprehensively persuading himself that she was capable of a 550-mile journey on foot. "The animal could succumb to fatigue: the failure of my enterprise would in no way be forgiven: but I accounted for all possible odds [with] firm resolution and confidence in the future."

The lists and orders, itineraries and invoices over the next twelve days record his flurry of preparations for Zarafa's convoy. It was still unusually cold in the north of France. It was warmer in the south but raining often. To protect and warm Zarafa, Saint-Hilaire commissioned an oilskin cloak to be tailored "for her body and her neck, in two pieces," bordered all around with a black braid. The order included a new collar for her. Worried that her hooves might wear down before journey's end, Saint-Hilaire foresaw that it might be necessary when they reached Lyon "to guarantee her hooves with boots."

The prefect reported to the professors in Paris that, while busy in Marseille, Saint-Hilaire visited the city's public collections and the private *cabinets de curiosités* "of persons who cultivate this genre of knowledge in this province and he responded to their desire to know the scientific names of a multitude of objects." Solicited by the doctors of Marseille, Saint-Hilaire also delivered an inspiring lecture at Salze's secondary school in which "he brought the professors and the students up to date on the novelties of anatomical science and his indefatigable kindness in this regard produced on this part of our population an impression the results of which can only bear fruit." And as at Montpellier, he was asked to speak to the scientific academies of Marseille and Toulon.

Grandly invoking the name of Professor Geoffroy Saint-Hilaire—"a sufficient indication of the interest that the government attaches to the preservation of these precious objects of natural history"—the prefect wrote to authorities along the route precautioning security against crowds and traffic. "The Giraffe is most gentle and can cause no accidents other than those occasioned by the shock of her gigantic body to draft animals who will be frightened at the sight of her." Relay squads of mounted gendarmes were requested to escort the convoy through their jurisdictions. The gendarmes were also asked to "keep the cows within reach of the conductors." Mayors in villages of projected nightly stops were instructed to designate stables with headroom of at least twelve to thirteen feet.

To simplify the logistics of getting Zarafa to Paris,

the Egyptian milk cow that had lost its milk was sold. Thanks to the zoological enthusiasm of the prefect, though, she was replaced by the male and now pregnant female mouflon. Saint-Hilaire had also planned to reduce "the baggage of the Giraffe" by leaving the male antelope and the feed it would need in Marseille, but seeing the animal's uniqueness changed his mind. Saint-Hilaire had never seen one like it and could only describe its resemblance to more familiar species of antelope: "The companion of the Giraffe turned out to be a very precious animal . . . new to zoology . . . even a new sub-species; for it unites the principal features of the gnu, the mouflon, and the antelope."

This animal was so new to Europe that its species had not yet been named. Saint-Hilaire dubbed the beast Sennari, after Sennar in central Africa, and described it to his colleagues in Paris as "robust and very mean." He had a solid cage built for it and contracted for a horse and carriage to transport it along with the cage of the two mouflon.

It was agreed that the carriage driver's daily salary would increase if the journey exceeded fifty days. His salary included an eight-day stay in Paris and his twelve-day return to Marseille. An invoice meticulously specified the costs of a carriage in good condition, new harness, and that the horse "proper to the carriage" was eight years old. As well as the caged animals, the driver would be responsible for hauling their feed supplies of barley and bran and maize and beans, which Saint-Hilaire had wanted to avoid but now bought in surplus to last until Lyon. The carriage would also bring the hide and skeleton of the female antelope, Saint-Hilaire's baggage, and the tack of four animal handlers. Driver and handlers received their salaries and "other outlays necessitated by their departure" in advance.

In addition to the carriage driver and Hassan and Atir, Saint-Hilaire signed on two other hands for the journey. One was Barthélemy Chouquet, a Marseillaise who first appears in the records as the man sent by the prefect to collect his cousin's mouflon. Curiously, Barthélemy's salary was twice that of Hassan, though the latter was the foreman in charge of the animals and their handlers and relied more on Atir.

The other addition to Zarafa's coterie was a young black French-Egyptian boy named Youssef Ebed. Youssef, Joseph to the French, was the son of refugees who had accompanied Napoleon's army back to France. Twenty-six years after the retreat, the Egyptians still lived in a refugee camp at Marseille, where Youssef was born and grew up bilingual.

The local military strictures on refugees required the prefect himself to notify the commandant of Youssef's departure for Paris. Without indicating his exact age, the records document that he was young enough for his welfare payments to be claimed by his father while he was away serving Saint-Hilaire as "aide and translator" to Hassan and Atir. Ebed, Joseph, Egyptian Refugee #487, was "entitled to a daily assistance of 72 centimes"—about twelve cents a day in 1827. Before their departure from Marseille, Saint-Hilaire advanced Youssef his entire salary of 43.25 francs, which was double the amount of his monthly welfare. His new mentor would also pay his expenses along the way.

The boy must have been excited to be a part of the impending adventure. This son of Egyptian refugees would see Paris with the king's giraffe. Neither Youssef nor any of the others, though, had any idea of the en-route renown that awaited the giraffe's procession. The crowds of the curious in Marseille turned out to be only an inkling of what was to come.

12

Misdemeanors of Curiosity

◡

VILLENEUVE-BARGEMONT advised to wait for sun, but Saint-Hilaire was determined to depart at the first possible moment.

At raining daybreak on the twentieth of May, sixteen days after Saint-Hilaire's arrival, Zarafa, bundled up in her new black-trimmed oilskins, followed the milk cows away from the prefecture for the last time. Hassan, as always, preceded with her lead rope. Atir and Barthélemy held ropes back to either side of her. She followed easily, restrained now by only three men, trained over the months of daily promenades by her desire to keep the milk cows in sight. It was a miserable Sunday morning. Church bells tolled as, instead of their usual good-weather route out into the countryside, the convoy began the long wet climb away from the sea.

True to thoughtful form, the prefect provided

Saint-Hilaire with a conversational companion for
this first day's march to Aix-en-Provence. The two
men led through the rain, followed by the milk cows
with their udders swinging ahead of Zarafa. Mounted
gendarmes escorted in advance and to the rear,
keeping their horses at a nervous distance from the
giraffe. Oncoming coaches and wagons and carts
were pulled off to the side of the road to avoid
frightening their teams while the procession passed.
Their drivers and passengers were treated to a
glimpse of strange horns in the cages on the carriage
and the astonishing sight of a giraffe in a raincoat.

Thanks to the doting care of the prefect, Zarafa

was strong and healthy and by far the least dis-
tressed member of her party. She was now nearly
full-grown, six inches taller than when she had arrived in Marseille, which put her height at exactly
twelve feet.

Saint-Hilaire had estimated that these initial
twenty miles to Aix would take eight hours, but he
found on the slow ascent "greater distance to reach,
a long rain, a group of people not yet shaped to the
demands of the trip and rather disposed to emanci-
pation." His exhausted apology to the prefect, written the next day from Aix, went on:

> It all proves the old saying that there is a God
> for innocents [like] the Giraffe. . . . Who is the
> extravagant [Saint-Hilaire] who put this beast
> en route in such bad weather? . . . In Paris
> they will without doubt believe me in the paths of
> negligence, because they view only the goal, they
> desire the Giraffe, and they are hardly disposed to
> value the difficulties. How much, Sir, I owe to
> you personally . . . concerning the Beautiful Afri-
> can . . . [and I] renew my promises to keep you
> informed . . . of this daughter of your affections
> and attentions.

The prefect had suggested that Zarafa's cloak be
adorned with the arms of France, but there had not
been time to do so before leaving Marseille. Saint-

Hilaire had the insignia embossed on the cloak while they rested the next day in Aix and, in a gesture of homage, asked the local authority to report this to the prefect in his account of the giraffe's visit: "The Giraffe is in perfect health. Mr. Geoffroy did a very great kindness for the population; Monday morning he had the Giraffe make a tour of the Cours and she was exposed for some time for people to see: a similar promenade took place in the evening at 7:00; the gathering of the curious was incredible."

Saint-Hilaire described the crowd under the tunnel of trees along the Cours Mirabeau at Aix—arching cathedral-high and ancient now, already old then—as "a cavalry charge." It was just before Ascension Day, and a religious procession delayed and seemed to consecrate the morning spectacle of the giraffe. "But the population was insatiable," Saint-Hilaire reported to the prefect, "and the Giraffe was more tired from these occupations of repose than she was from the day's march."

During that day of rest, it was also necessary to satisfy the more discreet curiosity of the local bourgeoisie. In Aix Saint-Hilaire thus learned immediately that both public and private performances would be required of Zarafa, a situation he described to the prefect as "double duty for the poor little girl, for this adopted daughter of your house."

The convoy left Aix on Tuesday at a less demanding 8:00 A.M., still climbing northwest through the

limestone hillsides and umbrella pines; but there was
sunshine in Saint-Hilaire's next letter to the prefect.
Three days from Aix, nearing Avignon: "Everyone
knows what he has to do and everyone is at their
post; I say that of all [of us,] beasts and people. The
Giraffe this morning at Orgon was calm under her
armorial cloak: as soon as she saw the cows in the
movement of departure, she left on her own, preced-
ing the order of her chief handler Hassan, glorious
as a peacock shunning her lead rope."

Atir held what was regarded (at least by Hassan
and Atir) as the second most important rope to her
right; Barthélemy was relegated to her left; Youssef
drove the milk cows. The rocky pine forests had
given way to orchards of almonds and olives and
cherries. There were wheat fields, green and yellow-
ing, spattered with red poppies. Bright yellow gorse
grew wild everywhere, and its scent filled the air,
sweet and musky. Locals tagged along, attracting curious magpies, stirring up insects for the swifts dart-
ing overhead.

Local notables and "friends of science" took
honored turns walking with Saint-Hilaire through
their districts. At each night's stop he would be officially greeted and invited to view the *cabinets de curiosités* of local physicians and veterinarians.

The medical men, knowing Saint-Hilaire's work
on genetic monstrosities, commemorated his visits
by presenting him with their prized specimens. "In

this regard, my harvest is abundant," Saint-Hilaire wrote to the prefect. "Two in Aix, one at St. Cannat, two in Lambesc: they give me these [monsters] with a generosity that is without example: the two from Lambesc interested me greatly: for me they are novelties that will one day be questions in the history of the sciences. I consider these benevolent windfalls reparation of this time lost, that is to say, not employed in the silence of the laboratory."

After the first four nights on the road, Saint-Hilaire joked to the prefect about needing him to save the convoy from greedy innkeepers, whom he described as "fleecers. . . . We pay for our coat of arms: The Beautiful Animal Of The King has, they say, a master well able to pay and they have also imagined to make me the Count of Saint-Hilaire." Another innkeeper spoke poetic truth, though, when he addressed Saint-Hilaire as "Comte de la Girafe."

At Avignon they rested for forty-eight hours before heading north up the valley of the Rhône. There were vineyards now, and after the agricultural market town of Orange with its Roman amphitheater, every rural village seemed the same, with gawking inhabitants and the mayor in his tricolor sash of office making a welcoming speech whether the convoy stopped there or not.

The countryside opened and flattened, and the unseasonably cold days along the Rhône were long and monotonous at Zarafa's two miles an hour. The warmer Mediterranean pulled cold wind, the mistral, out of the north. Behind the convoy, as the mistral blew in their faces, the north side of every house and building was blank, constructed without windows or doors because of the terrible wind called "the master" of the Rhône Valley.

The two-hour rest at midday was disturbed by crowds who were increasing as word of the giraffe preceded her. Saint-Hilaire reported that he was "busied in this regard by all persons along the route and who came out from surrounding cottages and chateaux alike."

Every afternoon, Saint-Hilaire had to hurry ahead to "debate and settle in advance the price of accommodation" at that night's stop:

> *Every evening, there were new concerns to prepare lodging for the Giraffe, which it was necessary [either] to find already suitable or to arrange, often in demolishment, by raising the roof of a stable. . . . In order that the animals transported by carriage could pass the night comfortably, they were taken from their cages every evening and returned to them every morning, which took time and required force and precautions. . . . [At] each arrival in populous towns . . . it was necessary to defend the Giraffe from the misdemeanors of indiscreet curiosity . . . and I had to fight the crowds who rushed tumultuously at the animal. This started afresh every day.*

Every night, after the crowds, Saint-Hilaire would have to entertain private audiences with the local gentry and officials, to whom he accorded "as amply as it was possible for me . . . the pleasure of contemplating the curious traveling animal at their ease."

They slept at Orange, Lapalud (where the mouflon lambed), Montélimar, Loriol . . . resuming each morning into the wind with or without rain, dealing with gawkers while proceeding on to the blank north side of every village and outlying farmhouse.

After Avignon, the first town of any size was Valence, where Saint-Hilaire was grateful for a letter from the prefect. Saint-Hilaire's friend Napoleon had attended the School of Artillery here as a sixteen-year-old cadet. Valence remained a military training center in Zarafa's time, as it is today, a town lively with girls and uniformed young men. Saint-Hilaire, fatigued and unwell at fifty-five, saw the recruits and must have remembered himself young with Napoleon. All his life, his son said, "the disasters of 1813–1814 . . . foreign invasion, the occupation of Paris, the fall of the great man whom he had known and loved in Egypt: such reversal of triumph overwhelmed him with a profound sadness."

Between Lyon and Valence, the steep course of the Rhône makes it fast and wild. Full of melted snow from the Alps, it shoots straight south churning green with whitecaps, and in spring the wind of it is like standing beside a fast train. As spring warms the valley of the Rhône and the temperature equalizes with Provence and the Mediterranean, the mistral dies out of the north.

That spring of 1827, however, was extraordinarily cold. Saint-Hilaire reported that during their seventeen days en route from Marseille to Lyon, "the convoy had to suffer two storms and several rainy days." As late as the first week of June, the rain turned to snow in the hills around Lyon.

Hassan and Atir had both seen the Nile flooded with summer rains, but it was nothing like this monster of ice water and wind called the Rhône. Before their winter in Marseille, they had never felt the northern cold, had never seen a dying season. Winter on the Nile was the time of planting and growing, and along it the landscape was constant desert.

Through the valley of the Rhône, though, the countryside kept changing. North of Valence, the road climbed from the blue distances of the south to the northern green of farms and far-off villages roofed with the same brick-red as the ribbon holding the amulet around Zarafa's neck. The land rolled out faceted into fields and vineyards and orchards and the vast tracts of mulberry trees—"the trees of gold"—that supported France's silk industry centered at Lyon.

At Tain on the first of June, a nail pierced the membrane between one of Zarafa's hooves. The nail was removed immediately and she was not limping, but Saint-Hilaire saw that she was weary from the past six continuous days of the march from Avignon. He decided to slow the pace and take six instead of four days to get from Valence to Lyon.

That night, instead of resting himself, Saint-Hilaire left a local doctor who was his former student in charge of the next day's march to St. Rambert and proceeded via mail coach "to organize the service of the curiosity of the great city of Lyon." He wanted also to implement a new plan, which he described in two letters sent the next day from Lyon. One letter was private, to his friend the prefect in Marseille. The other letter was official, to the minister of the interior in Paris.

At Lyon, as at Khartoum, two very different rivers meet. The Rhône crashes down from the east out of the Alps and overpowers the placid and darker Saône flowing into the city from the north. Saint-Hilaire's new plan was to avoid the crowds and the debilitating rigors of the march by sailing up the easily navigable Saône. As he wrote to the minister of the interior:

> *The Giraffe continues to enjoy perfect health . . .*
> *she has courageously endured the fatigues of the*
> *. . . 166 miles from Marseille to Tain . . . but*
> *she is feeling their effects, the cows are beginning*
> *to tire and one born in Egypt is limping a little.*
> *. . . I cannot conceal that the journey has in the*

*long run brought a dominant fatigue [to the gi-
raffe also], an uneasiness in all the movements of
the animal. . . . .[And] in the interest of the
health of the animal confided to me by the pa-
tronage of Your Excellency . . . I have seen that
the quays, the landings, and the boats [of the
Saône are] suitable . . . to the Giraffe who becomes more and more manageable and who, with
increasing docility and domestic education, has
the manners of the horse and the camel [enabling
her] to embark and debark by water from Lyon to
Chalon. The expense will be only a third more
than the route by land.*

In this letter Saint-Hilaire also suggested that,
nearing Paris, the giraffe be given a repose of eight
to ten days before she would be subjected

*to the ardent curiosity of the capital. If the King
could permit the animal to be received in the
stables of his palace at Fontainebleau, which
would expose her to the opportunity to be seen
sooner by His Majesty and the members of his
august family, I would detour the convoy. . . .
[All of the above] will preclude present plans and
must be prescribed by Your Excellency: if, to the
contrary, I receive no order, I will follow on
through Burgundy as planned. After debarking at
Chalon, I will submit an itinerary of the remain-*

*der of the route to Your Excellency; and if I am
authorized [to proceed by the Saône] I shall de-
vote myself [to that end] with zeal and punctu-
ality.*

Saint-Hilaire's letter to the prefect confided
uncle-to-uncle concern and pride, describing Zarafa's fatigue and affectionately recalling her shyness at
drinking her milk in front of strangers: "You would
not believe how . . . she is manageable, in a delightful
manner with perfect obedience. At l'Oriol in the evening and the next morning she drank her cup of milk
very bravely before the entire company and she now
no longer acts up [but she is] fatigued and it is better
to take precautions than to administer remedies."

Anticipating approval of his new plan by the minister of the interior, Saint-Hilaire had already arranged to sail the convoy up the Saône when he
mailed his letters and hurried back to St. Rambert
that night. The convoy was still three days south of
Lyon, where they would arrive on the fifth of June
and try to rest before embarking on the morning of
the ninth. During the four-day voyage to Chalon, the
crowds would get no closer than the riverbanks.

13

A Beautiful
Stranger

ZARAFA ENTERED LYON on schedule on Tuesday, June 5, 1827. That same day, Athens fell to the Turks. Since March, Muhammad Ali's French-trained forces had routed the previously victorious Greeks in battle after battle. While the viceroy was on his way to becoming the most unpopular man in Europe, in Lyon the newspapers suddenly made his giraffe the most famous thing in France.

One newspaper reported:

> Today the Giraffe toured a part of the city, accompanied by her keepers, a numerous picket of police, and a great crowd of the curious. The courteous animal did not fail to visit the Prefect, who accorded her the welcome due to a beautiful

*stranger. In order to protect her from the cold
temperature, she was dressed in a mantle of waxed
taffeta. The extraordinary temperature that has
afflicted us for several days seems to redouble its
rigor. Today the cold was so intense that snow fell
on the heights near Lyon.*

Saint-Hilaire recorded that while they were in
Lyon, the temperature fell below forty-three degrees
Fahrenheit.

The newspapers ran daily reports and a long two-
part essay on the giraffe by Saint-Hilaire, who also
received praising reviews for his inspirational address
to local students.

Lyon was interesting that week. Besides Zarafa
and her exotic retinue—on view twice a day under
the magnificent linden trees at the south side of the
huge place Bellecour, "along the promenade of the
flower sellers"—there was a grisly murder-suicide
and an execution at which "all the convicts were
present," a deterrent that caused the newspaper re-
porter to editorialize on the necessity of substituting
"in our penal laws a system of correction for a system of vengeance."

Also that week at la place Bellecour, the papers
advertised:

*Messrs. Gulley and Smitt, of London, have the
honor to offer to the public a superb collection of*

living serpents . . . every day from 11 in the morning to 8 in the evening, and composed of the following:

1. *The Rattlesnake, the only one to appear in France in the last 25 years;*
2. *The Serpent of Anaconda;*
3. *The Boa Constrictor;*
4. *The Embroidered Serpent;*
5. *The Harlequin Serpent.*

In addition, two Crocodiles of the Nile; the head of an Indian chief. . . . One is also able to see there a Giant, 6' 6" tall, aged 18 years. . . . The serpents are fed every Thursday at 3 P.M.

Saint-Hilaire, ringmaster of his own traveling circus, waited for permission from Paris to proceed up the Saône, socializing, distracting himself most enjoyably in the *cabinet de curiosités* "of the excellent and most learned . . . Director of the Veterinary School of Lyon, where I found a polydactyl monstrosity in a species of horse."

Meanwhile, the monstrous crowd in la place Bellecour quickly grew as people came again and again and brought their families and friends to see Zarafa on her morning and evening promenades. The mounted police became insufficient to control them and had to be augmented by military cavalry. As a precaution, Youssef had been promoted to help restrain Zarafa with a fourth lead rope.

The population of Lyon, like Marseille, was close to 100,000. Lyon, though, had the immense public space of la place Bellecour, which, on Friday morning after two days of press coverage and word of mouth, filled with 30,000 people eager to see the giraffe. Among them was a local celebrity, "the old woman of 113 years, who waited two hours patiently on a park bench." Messrs. Gulley and Smitt must have been busy arousing the serpents from their postfeeding lassitude, poking the rattlesnake into a fine rage for the audience they hoped to skim their way that day.

Zarafa made her appearance in the Bellecour at eleven o'clock, reportedly unperturbed in the beginning by what was far and away the largest of all the exhausting crowds she encountered before Paris. She was said to have calmly browsed the leaves of the linden trees overhead, amazing those close enough to see her prehensile tongue, blue-black and twenty inches long. As usual, the horses of her escort were skittish of her, but here the problem was ignited by claustrophobia. Caught between the strange creature and the crush of the crowd, one of the horses panicked and Zarafa bolted, dragging her handlers. The newspaper account blamed the ensuing riot on the soldiers who "without regard for the crowd, gave chase to stop her at a gallop and knocked down several persons, among whom especially was the honorable Mr. Geoffroy Saint-Hilaire."

Zarafa was promenaded again that evening, after

which there was another mishap in the crowd remaining in the Bellecour. The next day's newspaper
concluded: "It occurred to one that the Prefect, who
found himself in the brawl of the morning, would
have recognized the danger of placing horsemen in
the middle of the gathering caused by the desire to
see the Giraffe; one was wrong, and this evening,
after this animal [left the Bellecour], a horse reared
in the middle of the throng and wounded several
persons more or less grievously. The Giraffe departs
tomorrow at 7 in the morning."

The day of her scheduled embarkation up the
Saône, that Saturday after the tumult, passed with no
word from Paris. Whatever the reasons, the minister
of the interior never responded to Saint-Hilaire's letter requesting the change of plans.

Ironically, Saint-Hilaire would have avoided Lyon
and its crowds to rest Zarafa if not for his expectation of sailing with her from there to Chalon. In his
letter of June 2 to the prefect in Marseille, he had
written, "If I had not judged her transport possible
by water, my plan was to sequester her for a week in
a remote countryside."

True to his word, though, Saint-Hilaire pushed
on overland through Burgundy. He claimed his
wounds in Lyon "were more numerous than grave,"
but they had to have aggravated his already worsening
gout and rheumatism. Worried for Zarafa and suffering himself, he shortened their daily marches. What-

ever he thought, seeing the Saône off to his right every day for almost a week, he kept private from even the prefect in Marseille. He apparently wrote to no one for the rest of the journey.

It was another Sunday when they left Lyon, twenty-one days since Saint-Hilaire had led his little circus out of Marseille. Paris had ignored him, but there was still time for the king to come to Fontaine-bleau.

14

True to His Word

⌒

THE ONLY APPARENT unkindness inflicted on Zarafa came from the wife of the dauphin, Madame la Duchesse d'Angoulême, whose rigid protocol kept the king from going to see his giraffe and needlessly lengthened her journey.

Marie-Thérèse-Charlotte de Bourbon—"Madame Royale," as she was known all her adult life—was the justifiably dour daughter of Louis XVI and Marie Antoinette. Her parents' marriage had remained unconsummated for seven years, due to the king's excruciating erectile pain caused by an abnormally tight foreskin. At last his brother-in-law, the emperor of Austria, traveled incognito to Paris to persuade him to undergo circumcision, after which all of France rejoiced at the queen's immediate pregnancy. Hoping for a male heir to the throne, though, even the mother was disappointed that this first child, born in 1778, was a girl.

In the summer of 1792, Marie-Thérèse was a young teenager when, before dawn on August 10, the Revolutionary mob attacked the Tuileries and slaughtered the palace guards and servants and even the kitchen staff. Arrested that day with her family, she was fourteen when winter came and her father was beheaded, fifteen when her mother followed him to the guillotine nine months later.

Their daughter remained in prison for three years—jailed in a former monastery, which caused Paris to call her "the Orphan of the Temple"— before being exiled to her mother's native Austria.

Marie-Thérèse d-Angoulême

The next year, to consolidate Bourbon political and diplomatic resources, she was married at eighteen to her twenty-one-year-old cousin, the duc d'An- goulême. He was the oldest son of her father's youngest brother—the man who had little expec- tation, until late in his life, of becoming King Charles X.

Marie-Thérèse lived the first nineteen years of her married life exiled with the French royal family in England. When the monarchy was restored in 1815, after a quarter of a century of bloody Revolu- tion and Napoleonic imperialism, Madame Royale was the most royal of the ultraroyalists, the most symbolic personage in all of France. She was childless and fat, nearing fifty the year Zarafa came to Paris.

Marie-Thérèse was so regal because she was not only descended from the Bourbon kings on her father's side—her father and her two uncles were all kings of France, and her husband, who was her blood relative, became the heir apparent—but her moth- er's lineage intricately related her to six centuries of Hapsburgs. Her sensitivity to matters of royal proto- col can be glimpsed in a gesture she made to her husband as they turned away from the deathbed of their uncle, King Louis XVIII, in 1824. As of that moment her husband suddenly outranked her as the new dauphin, and for the first time in their lives, either as childhood cousins or as adult spouses, Ma- dame Royale allowed him to walk in front of her.

Charles-Philippe de Bourbon, who became King Charles X, was the youngest of four royal sons. By the time Charles-Philippe was ten years old, his oldest brother and his father and mother had died. The five remaining siblings were raised at the court of their grandfather, King Louis XV. All three princes became kings of France. Charles-Philippe's youngest sister and oldest brother, who became King Louis XVI, were both beheaded during the French Revolution.

Charles-Philippe was in his early thirties when the Revolution drove him into exile. He was nearly sixty when the restoration of the monarchy allowed

Charles X

his return to France; sixty-seven when he became king; seventy-two when he was forced to abdicate and return to exile in England. He was tall and elegantly handsome all his life. At fifteen, he had been dissuaded from his enthusiasm for soldiering by one of his grandfather's ministers, who had told him, "That is unbefitting of a prince. Amuse yourself otherwise: beget debts and we will pay them."

Although married by royal arrangement to a daughter of the king of Savoy, Charles-Philippe remained faithful to his mistress all his life. This woman, Louise de Polastron, accompanied him into exile in 1789. She died in England in 1804; he outlived her by thirty-two years, devoted to her memory. For the rest of his life, Marie-Thérèse ran his household.

As king, Charles X affected a military simplicity in his daily life. He loved nothing better than to spend the day anonymously hunting rabbits in the royal forest at Fontainebleau. Dressed as a commoner and on foot, accompanied only by his dog, it amused him to be accepted by poachers as one of their own. He was such a likable stranger that he was once asked to serve as godfather at a christening, where not even the priest recognized the man who identified himself as Mr. Leroy, Charles.

THE KING'S MINISTERS kept him apprised of the giraffe's progress from Marseille toward Paris. As the crowds and excitement grew around her, the king complained that he would be the last person in France to see his own giraffe. And this was exactly the protocol demanded by Madame Royale, who argued that kingly decorum obliged His Highness to wait and receive and not rush out to greet this gift from a lesser monarch.

En route from Lyon, Saint-Hilaire received no response at all to his request to detour and rest the giraffe at Fontainebleau.

The convoy pushed on through Burgundy, up the ancient Roman road between the Saône on their right and, on their left, the rolling foothills stitched with vineyards initiated by Caesar's legionnaires who retired here after conquering Gaul in the first century A.D.——eighty straight miles through villages whose eponymous wines are now the royalty of France.

At Chalon, the road slowed climbing northwest away from the Saône. Vineyards rose into woods and the hedgerows and green pastures of remote mountain hamlets. After Lyon, where Saint-Hilaire's correspondence ended, there was no further night-by-night record of their stops. Saint-Hilaire's painful gout and rheumatism were now compounded by an onset of uremia, causing him to spend more and more of each day riding with the caged animals on the carriage.

The jacket of this book reproduces an eyewitness painting of the convoy on the road over these moun-

tains near Arnay-le-Duc. The giraffe in the painting
steps sprightly and gaily attended by her handlers
while, in the distance ahead, Saint-Hilaire is a shadowy figure isolated on the rear of the carriage, seated
facing backward. Here the road wound through forests, down and up and down the long gradual water-
shed of the Seine.

The painting belies the general fatigue of the
convoy after Lyon. Squabbles erupted among the
men, which Saint-Hilaire later described officially to
the museum and privately to the prefect. His official
version mentions no names: "It was necessary to
marshal the duty of men of very different nationality,
religion, language, and character, to lead them to de-
liver in concert their strength and industry in the
service of the Giraffe, to intervene fairly often [in
their] bitter combats and continual struggles."

But writing from Paris to the prefect in Marseille
weeks later, Saint-Hilaire identified the problem as
Barthélemy. In sharp contrast to the grateful affection Saint-Hilaire felt for Hassan and Atir, he
described Barthélemy as an opportunistic and argu-
mentative blowhard.

We know the convoy stopped in Auxerre, because Saint-Hilaire's very worried twenty-one-year-
old son met him there on his own way south and
wrote home to his mother on June 23:

> *Between Joigny and Auxerre, my anxiety*
> *worsened: alone in the carriage, I, who never*

cries, had a sobbing fit: for, having found no authorities at Joigny knowing of the arrival of the Giraffe, I conceived the idea that Papa had been unable to endure the journey and had not arrived at Auxerre. I learned a little before Auxerre that the Giraffe was there and immediately upon my arrival ran to where she was lodged: Papa was not quartered there, but I soon learned where he was and someone took me to him. I found him . . . pale, but he seemed nevertheless in good enough health. . . . Hardly had I arrived when it was necessary to go and dine at the home of a Monsieur whom I do not know: I was seated at the other end of the table from Papa and . . . the whole time I felt ready to cry at . . . finding myself thus separated from him at the moment of my reunion with him, and at the thought that he was going to leave me tomorrow morning.

Meanwhile, the fall of Athens had motivated the European powers to intervene in Greece. On June 26 newspapers reported that France had allied with Britain and Russia in issuing an ultimatum of peace to the sultan in Constantinople: "At last the cries of the Greeks' bloody agony have touched the hearts of the Christian Kings." A combined fleet of warships from all three countries would sail for Greece "to separate the combatants" and enforce Europe's mediation.

While France and the rest of Europe reacted to

the news of this Enlightenment Crusade against the Turks, Zarafa and the convoy struck the Seine at Montereau, where they did not, as Saint-Hilaire had hoped they would, detour west to the palace at Fontainebleau.

Thirty miles and two days later, they were close enough to Paris for Saint-Hilaire's friend Marie-Henri Beyle, better known as Stendhal, to organize a boating party up the Seine to see the giraffe. On Saturday, June 30, Beyle and his party of young women—he was courting the stepdaughter of Cuvier, Saint-Hilaire's great colleague and rival; and she, like Zarafa, required chaperoning—sailed leisurely by steamboat to Villeneuve-St.-George, where Saint-Hilaire was expected to arrive that evening. But the convoy was a day ahead of schedule and was already entering Paris at five o'clock that same afternoon.

LYON TO PARIS HAD TAKEN them twenty-one days, including one day of rest. Before that, they had marched fourteen of their seventeen days from Marseille to Lyon. With a total of seven days' rest en route, Zarafa had walked 550 miles from Marseille to Paris in 41 days. Saint-Hilaire had slowed their pace before they reached Lyon, but over the entire journey she averaged sixteen miles a day.

When they reached Paris, Saint-Hilaire's only comment was his loving official report:

The health of the animals was in no way altered during the journey: on the contrary, [their health] is notably strengthened. A female mouflon lambed at Lapalud and the baby well endured the journey.

But it is principally the Giraffe whom the journey has marvelously benefited. She gained weight and much more strength from the exercise: her muscles were more defined, her coat smoother and glossier upon her arrival here than they were in Marseille: she is presently 12' 2" tall. Also during the journey, her ways became more trusting: she no longer refuses to drink in front of strangers; and her complacency with the play of the little mouflon, which [while resting off her feet, the giraffe] accepted on her back, testifies that she is as debonaire as she is intelligent.

15

The Degree of Happiness

⌒

ZARAFA WAS temporarily installed in a greenhouse on the grounds of le Jardin du Roi (again renamed le Jardin des Plantes after the monarchy was finally abolished in 1848).

The king was nine miles away, overlooking Paris from the palace at Saint-Cloud. He wanted to see his giraffe, and orders were issued for troops to escort his carriage to le Jardin du Roi on the coming Thursday.

In his official report, Saint-Hilaire wrote that his own health was nowhere near as good as the giraffe's: "In the face of many different duties, I was finally overcome by the excess of fatigue: toward the end of the journey I developed a very grave malady." He identified this malady to the prefect as an acutely painful retention of urine caused by blockage of the urethra, from which he was still convalescing weeks later.

But neither the king's eagerness nor Saint-Hilaire's illness, nor even the fact that the giraffe had just walked 550 miles, mattered to Madame Royale. In Saint-Hilaire's words: "Madame la Dauphine saw differently and believed it more dignified for the King not to displace himself; she came [to le Jardin du Roi] . . . and, having interrogated me, was decided." And so the royal plans were changed: On the morning of Monday, July 9, the giraffe would be paraded through the city to Saint-Cloud, where she would be received by the king.

Crowds filled the streets that day and followed along as Saint-Hilaire and his museum colleagues and Barthélemy, Youssef, Atir, and Hassan, with an escort of royal cavalry, walked Zarafa across Paris to meet the king. The newspaper account glosses the gratuitous ordeal between the lines:

> *Yesterday, at 10:00 in the morning, the giraffe, having left Paris at 6:00, arrived [outside the palace] greenhouse at Saint-Cloud, conducted there through the Trocadero. A numerous crowd of curious accompanied her.*
>
> *A deputation of the Institute, composed of Messrs. Cuvier, Geoffroy-Saint-Hilaire, and all the members of the administration of le Jardin du Roi [also accompanied] to present the animal to*

The giraffe being presented to the king at Saint-Cloud

the King, and to explain its habits and character to him. This deputation had the honor of being presented to the King before Mass by His Excellency, the Minister of the Interior.

At noon, the King, the Dauphin, Madame la Dauphine, Madame la Duchesse de Berri, and the princes of France, accompanied and followed by the entire court, betook themselves [outside], and Mr. Geoffroy-Saint-Hilaire had the honor of presenting to the King the gift of the Pasha of Egypt, as well as a pamphlet on the giraffe that he had written, and in which the story of this animal is described with care and exactitude.

His Majesty wished to see this singular quad-

ruped walk and even to run; the entire court was present and her gaits, especially running, appeared completely extraordinary. For more than half an hour, the King interrogated the learned academician. His Majesty appeared very satisfied with [Saint-Hilaire's] responses and deigned to show all his satisfaction to him.

At three o'clock, the giraffe returned to Paris, where she arrived safe and sound with her cortege. A crowd of curious followed her all the way to le Jardin du Roi.

Not counting the command performance of her gallop, it was an eighteen-mile day—6:00 A.M. to 7:00 P.M.—longer than any of her thirty-four traveling days en route from Marseille. And, of course, Saint-Hilaire's letter to the prefect tells more:

I dragged myself to Saint-Cloud and, paying attention to my pains, asking them what I ought to do—if I should step forward, if I should draw back—I took it squarely upon myself and it appears that I was able to satisfy the burden of the audience [with the King], which fell entirely on me and which could have been shared by some of my colleagues who were all present. But the King, to whose attention Madame la Dauphine brought me, spoke solely to me for an entire hour and took much pleasure indeed in the details and ideas of the organization of creatures that I min-

gled in my responses. The King inquired of the
manner in which I had commenced my mission,
which furnished me with the opportunity to speak
to him of [you, Villeneuve-Bargemont,] and I
informed him of the plenitude of my sentiments
for the kindnesses with which I was honored [by
you] in Marseille. [During the event] the Giraffe
exhibited all the graciousness of which she was
capable. . . . The King wanted details about the
Giraffe's team of handlers: I called his attention
to Hassan, who had already conducted a male
Giraffe to Constantinople; and to the negro Atir,
formerly the slave of Mr. Drovetti. [The King]
went to see the Minister of the Interior to order
him to send in the evening 2,000 francs to Hassan and 1,000 to Atir: this was executed to the
great contentment of both. The two other handlers, Barthélemy and the negro boy Youssef, will
be thanked [on July 12] by the administration
of le Jardin du Roi. The administration will allo-
cate them very sufficient means of returning [to
Marseille]. . . . The mail will bring you the pamphlet that I wrote for the King, of which I printed
only 30 copies. My artists are hard at work repro-
ducing the Giraffe.

And so was everyone else as she became the rage
of Paris. En route from Marseille, villages had named
streets and squares Girafe to commemorate her pas-

sage. Even taverns and inns not along her way were named for her, as provincial proprietors all over France either heard of her or saw her at the zoo in Paris and went home and renamed their establishments.

After being received by the king, Zarafa was put on daily public exhibition at le Jardin du Roi. In the last three weeks of July 1827, 60,000 people came to see her. She was soon the subject of songs and instrumental music, poems and vaudeville skits, and anonymous political satires criticizing the king's censorship of the press. Unlike her short-lived companion in London, Zarafa became a tool but never the object of journalistic ridicule. Paris adored her.

Children playing in the parks of Paris bought

Admission ticket to view the giraffe at le Jardin des Plantes snacks of gingerbread giraffes. Their mothers wore their hair *à la Girafe*, coiffured so high that they had to ride on the floors of their carriages. That summer the *Journal of Women and Fashion* reported the chic of "a necklace *à la Girafe*, a narrow ribbon from which is suspended a pink heart or better yet a small locket of the seraglio in the form of the amulet seen around the neck of the Giraffe at le Jardin du Roi."

The most stylish colors of that year's fashion season were "belly of Giraffe," "Giraffe in love," "Giraffe in exile." Men wore "Giraffic" hats and ties, and a magazine of the day diagrammed instructions for tying a gentleman's cravat *à la Girafe*.

Zarafamania was everywhere—in textiles and

The giraffe appeared on products everywhere

wallpaper, crockery and knickknacks, soap, furni-
ture, topiary—anywhere her distinctive spots or
long-necked shape could be employed. The recently
invented claviharp was renamed the "piano-Giraffe."
That winter's influenza was "Giraffe flu"; and people
inquired of the sick, "How goes the Giraffe?"

One of Saint-Hilaire's colleagues, naturalist Bory
de Saint-Vincent, was in a Paris debtors' prison at
the time and pleaded with the court—"in the name
of science"—for special leave to view the giraffe. His
request was denied. But the roof of his prison looked
down on the highest point in le Jardin du Roi, where
his friends at the museum arranged for Zarafa to be
seen by him telescopically.

Hassan stayed on in Paris until the end of October. En route back to Egypt, he delivered Saint-
Hilaire's letter to the prefect in Marseille:

*Hassan is leaving us . . . with a gift of 2,000
francs from the King. We have treated him with
consideration [and] he has merited our attention:
for he has stayed truly and faithfully with his
animal. He leaves in bad shape physically . . .
and, I think, in a chronic state of depression.
God will have pity on him one way or another.
We gave him 226 francs, one for every league of
his return to Toulon [in addition to his 2,000
francs from the King]. I would be flattered, Sir,
if you would confirm to him the affections that
we have already expressed to him.*

Atir remained with Zarafa, and they took up residence together in one of the five radiating, hexagonal, two-story alcoves of la Rotonde. The distinctively shaped building had been completed in 1805 as an architectural replica of the pentacular cross of the Legion of Honor—another of Zarafa's links to Napoleon, who created the award in 1802 and designed the cross himself to honor excellence in whomever he found possessed it, part of his intention to establish an aristocracy of achievement.

"Her winter apartment," as Saint-Hilaire described Zarafa's alcove to the prefect, was floored with parquet and insulated with an "elegant mosaic" of straw matting on the walls. Opposite sets of double doors provided access either outside or into the center of the building, which was heated with stoves and the body heat of other animals as needed. "It is truly the boudoir of a little lady. . . . Atir arrives at his bed by two ladders . . . : the two characters visit each other, the Giraffe and Atir, head to head in the high spaces of the enclosure."

Atir greatly enjoyed his renown as Zarafa's handler, exhibiting her every day to the crowds, then publicly grooming her with a currycomb attached to a long pole. This proud but laborious daily ritual became part of the vernacular of Paris in a common expression of reluctance, "Do that or comb the Giraffe."

Long after they were gone, Atir and Zarafa still

Formal portrait of the giraffe and Atir by Nicolas Huet

lived in the memory and speech of those who had seen them. Gustave Flaubert was four years old when Zarafa arrived in France; as a child, he visited Paris from his native Rouen and saw her in le Jardin; over thirty years later he wrote in a letter to his friend, George Sand, that he was "as tired as the Turk with the giraffe."

Saint-Hilaire was amused by Atir's other reputation as a ladies' man, reporting to the prefect: "He is a true French chevalier with good luck: he causes talk; for Madame la Duchesse de Berri wanted me to confide to her ears some of his adventures or misadventures. Among princesses, these things enter by one ear but pass quickly out the other."

France's other exotic highlights that summer included a whale washed up on the beach at Ostend on the Belgian coast and, in Paris, six Osage Indians from America. A newspaper reported:

> Chief Little Prince of Blood has distinguished himself in several combats and taken several scalps of his enemies . . . [a young brave named] Black Spirit appears to be his confidant. [When the] savages from Missouri arrived at Le Havre . . . people shoved and crowded neither more nor less than Parisians for the Giraffe. The Chief and his companions went to the theatre . . . in costumes a little less uncovered [than during the day]. The countenances of the Indian braves were rather

bothered, and the performance appeared not to interest them greatly; the Indian women had better bearing and seemed more attentive. Artists were seen drawing their costumes, without doubt to send them to Paris. We shall soon have fashions à la Missouri.

In Paris, Saint-Hilaire described the Indian attack on Zarafa's box office: "We were threatened with being overrun by the Osage, but we fought them off. It is all the rage now to see the red men, but the Giraffe continues to be very much courted."

Honoré de Balzac (who dedicated his novel *Père Goriot* to his friend Saint-Hilaire) was one of her suitors and published a pamphlet titled: "The Discourse of the Giraffe with the Chief of the Six Osages (or Indians) on the Occasion of Their Visit to le Jardin du Roi, Translated from the Arabic by the Giraffe's Interpreter." Forty thousand people bought tickets to see Zarafa that August. Her combined 100,000 visitors during July and August represented one-eighth of the entire population of Paris.

This was an immeasurably better summer than Messrs. Gulley and Smitt were having. In Lyon, one of their serpents had died, which inspired the enterprising Englishmen to postpone their closing day in order "to allow the public to view the animal in a way that is impossible when it is living, and to give amateurs the occasion to study this terrible reptile without danger." At the end of July, the Messrs. were denied entry into Switzerland by a magistrate who ruled that their traveling serpentarium was intended "only to serve the speculation of the proprietors and to satisfy a vain curiosity" of the public. The magistrate's ruling also reasoned that the rattlesnake was "small, and if it managed to escape, could easily hide, survive, and propagate in our regions."

ON JULY 6, within a week of Zarafa's goodwill arrival in Paris and three days before her reception by the king at Saint-Cloud, the European powers had signed their treaty against Muhammad Ali and the Turks. While the ships of the alliance were en route to Greece, Drovetti sailed for France on a mission for Muhammad Ali: Wishing to disassociate himself from his Turkish masters, the viceroy was offering to withdraw his forces from Greece in exchange for his own alliance with France against the sultan.

In a coincidence as amazing as any connected to the giraffe (and which Drovetti seems to have been so capable of arranging), Paris was at the height of Zarafamania when the consul general arrived from Egypt in late July.

His diplomatic mission was pointless. Despite the viceroy's offer to switch sides, his fleet set sail in August to reinforce the army commanded by his son at the Greek port of Navarino. Early in September, the sultan rejected the European ultimatum of mediation and continued the war. At Navarino, Muhammad Ali's son, whose chief of staff was Colonel Sèves, ignored demands from the alliance to cease off-loading troops and provisions. On October 20, the combined European naval force sailed into the port and destroyed the Egyptian fleet. The operation started around 2:30 P.M.; by 6:00, with no European losses, the Turks had lost Greece after all.

But Drovetti did very, very well for himself. Visiting Atir and Zarafa, he enjoyed the crowds at le Jardin and congratulated Saint-Hilaire on the zoo's historic and most profitable success. In return, Saint-Hilaire and his colleagues at the museum acknowledged the great debt that they felt science owed Drovetti for this giraffe whose "strength and health leave nothing to be desired."

And Drovetti availed himself of royal gratitude by selling the king his second collection of Egyptian antiquities, recently amassed and fortuitously coinciding with Zarafa's arrival in Paris. Champollion, on behalf of the Louvre, ensured the purchase with an authoritative recommendation. Total payment of the enormous price—after expert evaluation that "will not be able to exceed the sum of 150,000 francs"—was spread out over the next three years, during which time Drovetti retired as French consul general in Egypt.

Drovetti returned to Alexandria that fall in

wealthy triumph, bearing with him an ornately framed portrait of the giraffe as a thank-you gift from Saint-Hilaire and the museum to the viceroy. Saint-Hilaire had also given Drovetti the last of the thirty copies of his pamphlet about the giraffe, describing the work as "perhaps not for a Pasha who reads nothing: but you might be able to pass it on to someone in Egypt whom you would like to please with the enjoyment of possessing it."

IN 1830 Charles X's tightening censorship of the press precipitated events that forced his abdication. Madame Royale, whose unyielding protocol had marched Zarafa and Saint-Hilaire eighteen unnecessary miles back and forth across Paris, accompanied the king and her husband and all their family and courtiers back to exile in Britain.

Among the exiles was Baron Damas, the minister of foreign affairs who had refused to pay the giraffe's expenses in France. This nobleman, a former general, had also served as Louis XVIII's minister of war. In Britain, he became the governor of the last dauphin of France, the little six-year-old Dieudonnée who met the giraffe outside the palace that day at Saint-Cloud and never became King Henri V.

Despite Charles X's anachronistic and politically fatal inability to compromise, his former subjects came to regard his brief reign with nostalgia. After the terrors of the Revolution and the devastating wars of the Napoleonic Empire, this handsome elderly survivor had presided over better times. The Enlightenment had trickled down to the man in the street, and, for a while, just being alive was fascinating enough. The mobs came not for blood but excited to see "savages from Missouri" or a giraffe and her Arabs.

There was time then—time for the king to be charming in the old way, and time for his subjects to enjoy themselves—time even for Stendhal, the great chronicler of Napoleonic glory and Restoration disillusionment, to day-sail up the Seine with a boatful of young women who missed seeing the giraffe but had their picnic anyway.

Stendhal had been embittered into self-imposed exile by Napoleon's demise in 1814. In 1821 Napoleon died and Stendhal came home to France. When the decade of Zarafa's arrival ended with another overthrow of a French king, the lifelong Bonapartist and master of literary self-analysis was moved to write: "It will perhaps take centuries for the rest of Europe to achieve the degree of happiness that France enjoyed under the reign of Charles X."

SAINT-HILAIRE RECOVERED HIS HEALTH, and he was there at le Jardin in 1839 when a second giraffe arrived as a companion for Zarafa.

Saint-Hilaire's sight failed the year before he re-

tired, in 1841, after forty-seven years as the museum's founding zoologist. He died at seventy-two in
1844, just before the summer solstice—that part of
June when his journey with the giraffe had been at
its most difficult. Decades after their emotional reunion in Auxerre, his son described Saint-Hilaire's
funeral: "This ceremony greatly impressed the
friends of science and of this savant. It was less a
funeral than the consecration of one of the glories of
our century . . . the most magnificent homage to
genius and to the truth."

It is curious—and may or may not be indicative
of how Saint-Hilaire's family felt about his ordeal
with Zarafa—that she is not mentioned in the son's
biography of his father.

Epilogue

FLOCKS OF migrating storks still circle Luxor Temple, an immemorial landmark in their long biannual journeys to and from Europe. When Zarafa and her companion sailed past Luxor Temple in the spring of 1826, there were two obelisks at its portal. We now know that the hieroglyphs carved on the obelisks acclaim the reign of Rameses II—"The chiefs of all lands are under thy sandals"—and that their tapering heights represent rays of the sun, not rising but emanating from their pointed tips down to earth. The two obelisks had stood together at Luxor while sand and rubble rose around them for more than 3,000 years. Moses may have seen them.

After weeks of excavation, on November 1, 1831, it took French engineers twenty-five minutes to lower the western obelisk (and six more weeks to drag it 450 feet to the Nile) for its journey as another gift from Muhammad Ali to France.

Muhammad Ali had originally given France an obelisk in Alexandria ("Cleopatra's Needle," now in New York City's Central Park). But Champollion, seeing the magnificent Luxor obelisks in 1829, wrote to Drovetti: "Have you responded yet on the project of removing the obelisk from Alexandria? I hope this letter arrives in time for you to suggest to Paris the better idea of having one of the obelisks of Luxor instead of the ragged unfortunate of the Ancient Port. It would be more worthy of [our] nation, of the Minister and of you."

Like Zarafa, the Luxor obelisk was separated from its companion and embarked for Paris. Muhammad Ali declared: "I have done nothing for France that France has not done for me. If I give her the debris of an ancient civilization, it is in exchange for the new civilization which she has planted in the East. May the Theban obelisk reach Paris safely and serve as a bond between these two cities for all eternity."

Champollion died a year before the obelisk arrived in Paris on December 23, 1833, which would have been his forty-third birthday. The obelisk remained for eight months on board the ship, *The Luxor,* that had been built expressly to bring it on the long voyage down the Nile and overseas to Le Havre

Raising the obelisk in la place de la Concorde

and up the Seine to the quay at le pont de la Concorde. In August 1834 the obelisk was unloaded onto the quay, where it stayed crated on its side for another two years. On October 25, 1836, the ancient monument was erected in la place de la Concorde, where the guillotine had stood during the Revolution.

The excavation of the obelisk had revealed statues of priapic baboons around its base—animals whose noisy dawn-greeting ritual made them the holy personification of Thoth, ancient Egyptian god of writing. The baboons accompanied the obelisk to Paris, but Louis-Philippe, the last king of France, considered them inappropriate for a public monument and consigned them to the Louvre. Instead, the base of the obelisk in Paris bears the legend of its provenance and erection before "an immense crowd," along with gilded schematic carvings that demonstrate how it was raised. We have no idea and can only conjecture how the ancient Egyptians accomplished the same feat.

Louis-Philippe reciprocated the gift of the obelisk by sending Muhammad Ali a filigreed, three-story clock tower that has never worked since it arrived in Cairo. Useless, but nonetheless symbolic of the viceroy's predilection for the French and all that they helped him to accomplish, this quintessentially Western gizmo was incorporated into the huge mosque he built as his monument to himself. While Paris traffic blasts around the Luxor obelisk in la place de la Concorde, "the gingerbread clock," topped with the Turkish crescent, stands among the minarets of the old barbarian's tomb.

IN THE 1830s Muhammad Ali conquered Syria and opened hostilities against his Ottoman masters. He was at the apogee of his international career in 1839, when Sèves's troops defeated the sultan's German-trained army and were poised to attack Constantinople itself. The viceroy hesitated, wanting not to antagonize Europe without assurance of French support, precipitating an international crisis that threatened war between Britain and France. In June 1840 France backed down from war with Britain

Muhammad Ali being advised by Colonel Campbell, the British consul general, to abandon his plans against the Turks, while the British fleet threatens Alexandria in the background

over Egypt and was coerced into another alliance with Russia against the viceroy. Without the French support that he had cultivated and counted on for decades—the gifts of Zarafa and the obelisk from Luxor had been episodes in that effort—Muhammad Ali was forced to reduce his huge French-trained military and give up Syria in exchange for hereditary rights to Egypt.

Colonel Sèves, who as a boy was disowned by his

parents, became like a son to the viceroy. He converted to Islam, adopted the name Soliman Pasha, made a fortune in mercenary service to Muhammad Ali, and never went home. Flaubert met him in Alexandria in 1849 and described him as "the most powerful man in Egypt, the terror of Constantinople."

Joussouf Boghos, Muhammad Ali's closest ally for forty years, died in sad retirement in 1844. His funeral in Cairo was immediate, simple, and unassuming. The viceroy, however, was furious when word reached him in Alexandria that his friend had been laid to rest without ceremony. "Donkey, brute . . ." began the letter in which he insulted and threatened and ordered the governor of Cairo to exhume Boghos and rebury him with the full military honors of a state funeral.

Muhammad Ali died in 1849, outliving Zarafa by four years. At the end he was lost in senility, induced, it was said, by the silver nitrate used to treat his chronic dysentery. Given his early life, however, and his reputed harem of 800 women, it could very well have been syphilitic dementia. In 1825 Boyer had reported that the viceroy often disappeared into his harem for three or four days at a time and that "he still drinks heavily and sacrifices too often to Venus; however, his conversation is lively and animated." As the viceroy deteriorated in the final decade of his life, his personal physician Dr. A. B. Clot—yet another French expatriate in Egypt—was constantly prescribing abstinence.

Muhammad Ali never wanted a canal at Suez, which he believed would (and did in 1882) rationalize a British invasion. The viceroy's heirs, after building the canal, reaped and squandered and bankrupted Egypt into a British protectorate. His dynasty of figurehead kings ended when the infant son of King Farouk I was deposed in 1953.

BERNARDINO DROVETTI died in 1852, also senile. Egyptology had made him rich, and he had retired as consul general and returned to Europe in 1829, soon after receiving Champollion's letter from Luxor. In 1836, Drovetti sold his small third collection of antiquities for 30,000 francs to the Egyptian Museum in Berlin. Living out his life in poor health, he divided his time between elegant Mediterranean winters in Nice and summers in Turin. He remained a contradiction—revered throughout Europe as a *grand ami* of science, while also the generous patriarch of a large and, according to his banker, ungrateful family.

ZARAFA LIVED nearly eighteen years in Paris. She was there in 1830 when Louis-Philippe, the citizen-king, was elected to replace Charles X. She was in Paris when that other vertical wonder, the obelisk, arrived after its own two-year journey from Luxor. Twelve days after it was finally erected in 1836, Charles X

died in his second exile. Zarafa was in Paris in 1837
when the first train in France left the city for the
western suburb of St.-Germain-en-Laye. Also that
year, l'Arc de Triomphe was finally completed,
thirty-one years after Napoleon had begun its construction to glorify his armies of the empire. Zarafa
was in Paris when, in 1840, Napoleon's coffin arrived from St. Helena and was paraded under l'Arc
to permanent entombment in les Invalides.

In 1828 a mate arrived for le Jardin's resident
elephant, drawing crowds that were disappointed in
their hopes of watching the pachyderms "found a
family." Zarafa, though, never had a mate. Except
for her reflection, fragmented in the panes of the tall

*The giraffe and elephants outside la Rotonde at
le Jardin des Plantes*

glass doors of her enclosure, she did not see her own kind for thirteen years. Then, for the last six years of her life, she lived in le Jardin with France's second giraffe. This younger female had also been captured as a calf, and it is known that she was brought down the Nile by boat. When she arrived in Paris in 1839—a gift from Muhammad Ali's physician, Dr. Clot—she was around the same age that Zarafa and her long-ago companion had been when they were separated in Alexandria.

Zarafa died on January 12, 1845, seven months after Saint-Hilaire. She was, as the French say, "naturalized" and stood for decades on display in the foyer of the museum at le Jardin des Plantes. As other giraffes came to pass their lives in le Jardin, they, too, were naturalized. Eventually, needing space, the museum farmed these stuffed giraffes out to provincial museums throughout France. Zarafa was thought to have been sent to Verdun and destroyed with its museum in World War I. French soldiers were said to have excavated what was left of her neck and head from the rubble and to have erected her overlooking their trenches as a dawn joke on the Germans.

But that was not Zarafa.

Today, conclusively identified by her markings in the paintings commissioned by Saint-Hilaire, she stands on the landing of a staircase in a museum in La Rochelle on the west coast of France.

Le Musée La Faille is an eccentric little gem of a municipal collection, formerly the mansion of a man whose one-room *cabinet de curiosités* grew to take over the entire house. Wanting to keep his collection intact, Mr. La Faille donated his mansion and miniature Jardin des Plantes to the city of La Rochelle during his lifetime. In 1782, shortly before he died, it was opened to the public. Since then it has evolved into a museum that not only honors the avid amateur fascinations of its creator but also memorializes the eighteenth-century Enlightenment spirit of the *cabinet de curiosités* in general. Oddities juxtapose into relationships that baffle and intrigue, as though one is wandering around inside a man's mind.

The camel ridden by Napoleon in Egypt used to be exhibited here with Zarafa but has since been transferred to the Napoleonic Museum on the isle of Elba. Empress Josephine's stuffed pet orangutan is downstairs, though, and upstairs half a dozen mummified and yo-yo–sized shrunken human heads can be seen along with a 300-year-old skeleton of the flightless and extinct dodo and the entire alimentary system of a vulture in formaldehyde.

The high walls of the staircase around Zarafa are covered with the museum's collection of dusty ungulate heads and skulls and horns in so many different twisting shapes and sizes—African dik-dik to North American moose—that they mesmerize like flames, kinetic variations on an evolutionary theme. Mounted down the banister from the upper floor, three massive hippopotamus skulls gape at the giraffe.

She was not any of these, neither prey nor predator, describable only in terms of other beasts, with her magical attachment to humans. Sophisticated scientists were smitten with her, one describing her as "of a gentleness without example . . . a child could conduct this gigantic animal with a little cord anywhere he wanted."

Even Saint-Hilaire, zoology's founding specialist in monstrosities of nature and "the mutual affection" between species, was mystified by the giraffe's uniqueness. Asking rhetorically, in his official report, "What is the purpose of the Giraffe?" the august scientist could only conclude with the collective wonder, "It is without doubt useless to explain how and why the nature of things was thus decided."

IF YOU GO to see Zarafa in La Rochelle, do not bear left through the ground floor of the museum. Bearing left leads to an antique wooden staircase, which, though beautiful, is not where she is. Go to your right out of the first room full of butterflies and on through fish and mollusks, past the skeletons of carnivores and primates and other mammals until you get to the fossilized prehistoric Italian crocodile. Then look up the wide stone stairs, and you will find her gazing down at you.

Imaginatively positioned, her head is tilted so that her huge black eyes seem to scrutinize your ascending approach. A plaque identifies her simply as "Giraffe from Sennar." Even with the added height of a platform beneath her, she is surprisingly small and delicate. Naively preserved before taxidermy became an art, she is now too fragile to travel. The tall windows behind her have been boarded up to protect her from further fading by the sun. Instead, an overhanging electric light gleams in her eyes and casts her shadow standing on the white wall beside her, and she is silhouetted there as though inside that tent aboard her felucca sailing down the Nile.

Acknowledgments

MY DISCOVERY of the remarkable story of this giraffe sent me first of all to Geneviève Boulinier. Madame Boulinier's business card identifies her as the press officer of France's National Museum of Natural History in Paris, but this description of her helpfulness is like saying that champagne is wet.

"There are perhaps three hundred scientists here at the museum," she told me. "Ask me anything and I'll get back to you."

My favorite reply from her found me in Luxor, Egypt: "Giraffe eyelashes do not grow in tufts, but individually." And one blue-gray rainy day in Paris, she toured me around le Jardin des Plantes pointing out trees old enough for the giraffe to have seen nearly two centuries ago.

Christopher Dickey, whom I am proud to call my brother and who travels the Third World as a journalist, was not laughing when he joked that my giraffe research in Sudan would identify me there as a spy. Along with my shots, I had received alarming warnings about travel to central Africa, including a lurid no-go recommendation from the U.S. State Department. Sudan has been at civil war since before its independence from Britain in 1956, and the Sudanese have lived under Islamic martial law since 1983. A diplomat from Khartoum had told me there were rumors that slavery still existed in the rebel-held south, but denied the government's alleged violations of human rights and support of international terrorists. Within months of my visit late in 1996, the civil war would surge north. The University of Khartoum would be closed and its 15,000 students exhorted to join the defending government forces.

The night before I left for Khartoum, Chris went through my small fortune of preventive medicines, reading the dosages and elaborating their targeted symptoms for me in horrific detail, assembling the vials on the table where they stayed after he finally said, "If you get sick, get well at home. Meanwhile, don't slow yourself down with side effects."

In Sudan people were friendly, but my stated quest for a long-ago giraffe inspired them always to trade the same initial nervous glance. Then the giraffe's story would charm and I was still suspect, but so ingeniously disguised as a fool that my listeners would scatter to search for the oldest man who might remember. Sometimes they kept me waiting for someone who never came. When luck at last took me to Professor Gaffar Mirghani at the University of Khartoum, and I told him I was lost retracing the undocumented African part of the giraffe's journey, he laughed and said, "I had exactly the same problems with my hippo!"

Then it was my turn to be charmed and invaluably educated by his detailed knowledge of Sudan and Islam and the origins of Khartoum, and by his story of a young hippopotamus that had sailed from Khartoum down the Nile to Alexandria in 1849 and on to London in the spring of 1850.

"*Sailed?* From Khartoum?"

"The boat was built with a huge basin filled with water, like a bathtub, and the little hippo stayed comfortably immersed for the entire voyage."

"But what about the six Cataracts from here through Nubia? Wasn't the river unnavigable until after Aswân?"

Thirdhand French translations of secondhand oral Arabic accounts had the giraffe trekking with a caravan across the Sahara, but Professor Mirghani smiled and told me, "The Nile solves your problems. They waited for spring, when the river starts to rise with the good wind, the beautiful wind from the south. The *haboob*. At each Cataract they unloaded your giraffe—as they did my hippo, emptying its basin of water to raise the boat—and in the spring the Nile rose deep enough for the current to help pull the boat over the rocks. Your giraffe did not have to walk across the desert."

In Luxor, Ray Johnson and his staff at Chicago House are among the heroes of Egyptology's last tragic phase, documenting 5,000 years of history even as it disappears.

"Do you know what the Rosetta stone is made of?" Ray asked me.

"Black basalt, isn't it?"

"Pink granite. Some friends of mine at the British Museum just cleaned a tiny bit of a corner of it, very carefully."

"What turned the whole thing black?"

"Touching."

After Africa, France was a paradise of firsthand historical documentation. The giraffe still lives in the archives of Marseille and Lyon and Paris. The guardians of these places, in their generous and heartening enthusiasm for my project, gave me a living glimpse of how France fell in love with the giraffe as she walked from Marseille to Paris. Tracking the giraffe from archive to archive, I was honored to relive something of the welcome accorded to the men who accompanied her.

None of this would have happened for me, though, and this book would not exist without three people to whom my gratitude is inexpressible: George Gibson, *il miglior fabbro;* Michael Carlisle, to the Blue Nile and back; and Dava Sobel, who brought us all together.

Art
Credits

⌒

The art in *Zarafa* is credited to the following sources:
Endpaper map and maps on pages 94–95 and 143:
© 1998 Jeffrey L. Ward. Page ii: painting by Nicolas
Huet, © Bibliothèque centrale M.N.H.N., Paris.
Page 14: map by Joan Emerson, from *The Blue Nile*
© 1962 by Alan Moorehead, Harper and Row. Pages
25, 28, 52, 54, and 59: Bibliothèque nationale de
France, Paris. Page 30: courtesy of Michael V. Carlisle. Page 33: from *Travels in Upper and Lower Egypt*
by Vivant Denon, published 1803. Page 43: illustra-
tion from *L'Egypte au XIXeme Siecle* by Edouard
Gouin, collection of the Brooklyn Museum of Art,
Wilbour Library of Egyptology. Page 46: from *Egypt,
Descriptive, Historical and Picturesque* by G. Ebers,
published 1887. Pages 66, 161, and 163: from
Charles X by Georges Bordonove, published in 1990
by Editions Pygmalion/Gerard Watelet, Paris. Page
79: painting by David Roberts from *David Roberts: A
Journey in Egypt,* published in 1994 by Casa Editrice

Bonechi: Florence, Italy. Page 81: from *The Animal World of the Pharaohs* by Patrick F. Houlihan, published in 1996 by the American University in Cairo Press. Pages 91, 172, and 176: from *une girafe pour le roi*, published in 1984 by Musee de L'ile-de-France. Page 107: from *Le Chateau d'If* by Paul Laget, published 1956. Pages 127, 175, and 194: © Bibliothèque centrale M.N.H.N., Paris. Page 179: reproduction of a painting by Nicholas Huet from The Sunny von Bulöw Collection © The Pierpont Morgan Library, New York. Page 189: painting by Francois Dubois. Page 191: lithograph by Louis Haghe after a painting by David Roberts, from the collection of R. G. Searight.

Index

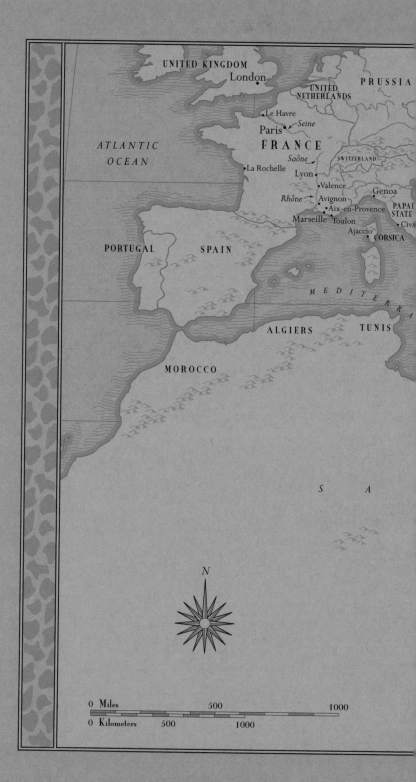